AMERICAN POLITICAL, ECONOMIC, AND SECURITY ISSUES

GOVERNMENT ACCESS AND COLLECTION OF PRIVATE INFORMATION

AMERICAN POLITICAL, ECONOMIC, AND SECURITY ISSUES

Additional books in this series can be found on Nova's website under the Series tab.

Additional E-books in this series can be found on Nova's website under the E-books tab.

AMERICAN POLITICAL, ECONOMIC, AND SECURITY ISSUES

GOVERNMENT ACCESS AND COLLECTION OF PRIVATE INFORMATION

COREY D. HEIMS
EDITOR

Nova Science Publishers, Inc.
New York

For permission to use material from this book please contact us:
Telephone 631-231-7269; Fax 631-231-8175
Web Site: http://www.novapublishers.com

LIBRARY OF CONGRESS CATALOGING-IN-PUBLICATION DATA

Government access and collection of private information / editor, Corey D. Heims.
p. cm.
Includes index.
ISBN 978-1-60876-085-5 (softcover)
1. Privacy, Right of--United States. 2. Records--Access control--United States. I. Heims, Corey D.
JC596.2.U5G68 2009
323.44'830973--dc22

2010025445

Published by Nova Science Publishers, Inc. † New York

CONTENTS

PREFACE

Shortly after the 9/11 terrorist attacks, Congress enacted the USA PATRIOT Act, in part, to provide enhanced investigative tools and to assist in the prevention of future terrorist activities and the preliminary acts and crimes which further such activities. To that end, the act eased restrictions on the government's ability to collect information regarding people's activities and conversations, both in domestic criminal investigations and in the realms of foreign intelligence gathering and national security. The changes are perceived by many to be necessary in light of the new breed of threats in a post 9/11 world. This book discusses the history of constitutional interpretations and legislative responses relevant to the collection of private information for criminal investigations, foreign intelligence gathering, and national security purposes.

Chapter 1- Public interest in the means by which the government may collect telephone call records has been raised by ongoing revelations regarding alleged intelligence activity by the National Security Agency (NSA) and the Federal Bureau of Investigation (FBI). According to a *USA Today* article from May 11, 2006, the NSA allegedly sought and obtained records of telephone numbers called and received from millions of telephones within the United States from three telephone service providers; a fourth reportedly refused to provide such records. Additionally, a series of reports issued by the Department of Justice's Office of the Inspector General (DOJ OIG), most recently in January of 2010, indicate that, between 2002 and 2006, consumer records held by telephone companies had been provided to the FBI through the use of "exigent letters" and other informal methods that fell outside of the national security letter (NSL) process embodied in statute and internal FBI policies.

Chapter 2 Congress enacted the USA PATRIOT Act soon after the 9/11 terrorist attacks. The most controversial sections of the act facilitate the federal government's collection of more information, from a greater number of sources, than had previously been authorized in criminal or foreign intelligence investigations. The Foreign Intelligence Surveillance Act (FISA), the Electronic Communications Privacy Act (ECPA), and the national security letter (NSL) statutes were all bolstered. With the changes came greater access to records showing an individual's spending and communication patterns as well as increased authority to intercept e-mail and telephone conversations and to search homes and businesses. In some cases, evidentiary standards required to obtain court approval for the collection of information were lowered. Other approaches included expanding the scope of information subject to search, adding flexibility to the methods by which information could be collected, and broadening the purposes for which information may be sought.

Chapter 3 This is a statement delivered as testimony given by Glenn A. Fine, Inspectore General, U.S. Department of Justice before the Senate Sub Committee on the Judiciary.

Chapter 4 This is a statement given by Lisa Graves, Executive Director for the Center for Media and Democracy before the United States Senate Judiciary Committee

In: Government Access and Collection of Private... ISBN: 978-1-60876-085-5
Editors: Corey D. Heims

Chapter 1

GOVERNMENT ACCESS TO PHONE CALLING ACTIVITY AND RELATED RECORDS: LEGAL AUTHORITIES

Elizabeth B. Bazan, Edward C. Liu and Gina Stevens

SUMMARY

Public interest in the means by which the government may collect telephone call records has been raised by ongoing revelations regarding alleged intelligence activity by the National Security Agency (NSA) and the Federal Bureau of Investigation (FBI). According to a *USA Today* article from May 11, 2006, the NSA allegedly sought and obtained records of telephone numbers called and received from millions of telephones within the United States from three telephone service providers; a fourth reportedly refused to provide such records. Additionally, a series of reports issued by the Department of Justice's Office of the Inspector General (DOJ OIG), most recently in January of 2010, indicate that, between 2002 and 2006, consumer records held by telephone companies had been provided to the FBI through the use of "exigent letters" and other informal methods that fell outside of the national security letter (NSL) process embodied in statute and internal FBI policies.

The Supreme Court has held that there is no Fourth Amendment protection of telephone calling records held in the hands of third party providers, where the content of any call is not intercepted. However, this report summarizes existing *statutory* authorities regarding access by the government, for either foreign intelligence or law enforcement purposes, to information related to telephone calling patterns or practices. Where pertinent, it also discusses statutory prohibitions against accessing or disclosing such information, along with relevant exceptions to those prohibitions.

Statutory provisions authorizing, pursuant to court order, the use of pen registers and trap and trace devices exist in both the Foreign Intelligence Surveillance Act (FISA), 50 U.S.C. § 1841 *et seq*., and, for law enforcement purposes, in 18 U.S.C. § 3121 *et seq*.

FISA's "business records" provision, 50 U.S.C. § 1861, provides authority, pursuant to court order, for requests for production of "any tangible thing" relevant to collection of foreign intelligence information not concerning a U.S. person, or relevant to an investigation into international terrorism or clandestine intelligence activities. Under 50 U.S.C. § 1861, an investigation concerning a U.S. person may not be based solely on activities protected by the First Amendment.

Access to stored electronic communications is addressed in 18 U.S.C. § 2701 *et seq.* 18 U.S.C. § 2702 prohibits voluntary disclosure of customer communications records by a service provider unless it falls within one of several exceptions. Required disclosure of customer records to the government under certain circumstances is addressed under 18 U.S.C. § 2703, including, among others, disclosure pursuant to a warrant or grand jury or trial subpoena. 18 U.S.C. § 2709 is a national security letter provision, under which a wire or electronic service provider may be compelled to provide subscriber information and toll billing records information, or electronic communication transactional records in its custody or possession.

Finally, § 222 of the Communications Act of 1934, as amended, protects customer proprietary network information, and violations of pertinent provisions of law or regulation may expose service providers to criminal sanctions, civil penalties, and forfeiture provisions.

Public interest in the means by which the government may collect telephone call records has been raised by ongoing revelations regarding alleged intelligence activity by the National PSecurity Agency (NSA) and the Federal Bureau of Investigation (FBI). According to a *USA Today* article from May 11, 2006, the NSA allegedly sought and obtained records of telephone numbers called and received from millions of telephones within the United States from three telephone service providers; a fourth reportedly refused to provide such records.[1] Additionally, a series of reports issued by the

Department of Justice's Office of the Inspector General (DOJ OIG), most recently in January of 2010, indicate that, between 2002 and 2006, consumer records held by telephone companies had been provided to the FBI through the use of "exigent letters" and other informal methods that fell outside of the national security letter (NSL) process embodied in statute and internal FBI policies.[2] These reports also indicate that records may have been sought without demonstrating a relationship to an active investigation.[3]

This report summarizes legal authorities regarding access by the government, for either foreign intelligence or law enforcement purposes, to information related to telephone calling patterns or practices. Where pertinent, it also discusses statutory prohibitions against accessing or disclosing such information, along with relevant exceptions to those prohibitions.

TELEPHONE RECORDS AND THE FOURTH AMENDMENT

The Supreme Court, in *Smith v. Maryland*, 442 U.S. 735 (1979), in a pen register case,[4] has held that there is no Fourth Amendment protected reasonable expectation of privacy in records of telephone calls held in the hands of third party providers, where the content of any call is not intercepted. The Fourth Amendment to the United States Constitution guarantees:

> The right of the people to be secure in their persons, houses, papers, and effects, against unreasonable searches and seizures, shall not be violated, and no Warrants shall issue, but upon probable cause, supported by Oath or affirmation, and particularly describing the place to be searched, and the persons or things to be seized.[5]

Whether the use of a pen register is a "search and seizure" within the meaning of the Fourth Amendment determines if the government, in compliance with the Constitution, must secure a warrant or court order prior to its installation. In 1979, the United States Supreme Court decided this question in *Smith v. Maryland,*[6] holding that the Fourth Amendment does not prohibit the use of pen registers without a warrant. Writing the majority opinion joined by four other justices, Justice Harry Blackmun drew a distinction between the acquisition of contents of telephone communications using electronic listening devices, which the Court in *Katz v. United States*[7] had deemed to be a "search" under the Fourth Amendment, and the capture of electronic impulses that identify the numbers dialed on a telephone using a pen register device.

According to the majority in *Smith*, it is a constitutionally significant difference that pen registers do not record the *contents* of communications, in contrast to the listening devices employed in *Katz*.[8] The Court explained that the Fourth Amendment does not apply to the use of pen registers because individuals do not have a legitimate expectation of privacy against invasion by government action, that protects the numbers dialed into a telephone system:

> All telephone users realize that they must "convey" phone numbers to the telephone company, since it is through telephone company switching equipment that their calls are completed. All subscribers realize, moreover, that the phone company has facilities for making permanent records of the numbers they dial, for they see a list of their long-distance (toll) calls on their monthly bills. In fact, pen registers and similar devices are routinely used by telephone companies "for the purposes of checking billing operations, detecting fraud, and preventing violations of law."[9]

The Court stated that telephone customers, by voluntarily conveying phone numbers to the telephone company and "expos[ing] that information to its equipment in the ordinary course of business," assume the risk that the company may disclose such information to law enforcement.[10] Because there is no actual or legitimate expectation of privacy in the numbers dialed from a telephone, the installation and use of a pen register is not a "search" requiring a warrant under the Fourth Amendment, the Court ruled.[11]

In contrast, the dissenting opinions in *Smith* concluded that telephone numbers dialed from a phone are entitled to the same constitutional protection that telephone conversations receive under *Katz* because such numbers are not without "content" - they "reveal the identities of the persons and the places called, and thus reveal the most intimate details of a person's life."[12] Furthermore, the dissenters objected to the majority's characterization that the use of a telephone involves an assumption of risk on the part of the customer that telephone dialing information might be disclosed to the government; assumption of risk generally requires there to have been a choice to engage in the activity, and "as a practical matter, individuals have no realistic alternative" to the use of a telephone.[13]

Although the protections of the Fourth Amendment may not reach records of telephone calls held by third parties, Congress has enacted a number of statutes since the *Smith* decision that both permit access by the government for foreign intelligence or law enforcement purposes to information relating to telephone numbers dialed from or received by a particular telephone number, as well as duration and usage, while simultaneously imposing limitations as to how such information may be accessed and under what circumstances it may be used.

STATUTORY PROVISIONS

Information regarding telephone calling patterns, duration, usage, and length of service may be sought by the government directly through the use of pen registers[14] or trap and trace devices.[15] Statutory provisions authorizing, pursuant to court order, the use of pen registers and trap and trace devices exist in both the Foreign Intelligence Surveillance Act (FISA), 50 U.S.C. § 1841 *et seq*., and, for law enforcement purposes, in 18 U.S.C. § 3121 *et seq*.

Telephone calling activity may also be collected indirectly by seeking telephone toll or transactional records from third party providers. For example, FISA's "business records" provision, 50 U.S.C. § 1861, authorizes court orders to compel the production of "any tangible thing" relevant to collection of foreign intelligence information not concerning a U.S. person, or relevant to an investigation into international terrorism or clandestine intelligence activities.[16]

Access to stored electronic communications is also addressed in 18 U.S.C. § 2701 *et seq.* 18 U.S.C. § 2702 prohibits voluntary disclosure of customer communications records by a service provider unless it falls within one of several exceptions. Required disclosure of customer records to the government under certain circumstances is addressed under 18 U.S.C. § 2703, including, among others, disclosure pursuant to a warrant or grand jury or trial subpoena. 18 U.S.C. § 2709 is a national security letter provision,[17] under which a wire or electronic service provider[18] may be compelled to provide subscriber information and toll billing records information, or electronic communication transactional records in its custody or possession in response to a request by the Director of the Federal Bureau of Investigation (FBI) if the Director of the FBI, or his designee in a position not lower than Deputy Assistant Director at Bureau headquarters or a Special Agent in Charge designated by the FBI Director in a field office, certifies that the records or information sought is relevant to an authorized investigation to protect against international terrorism or clandestine intelligence activities, provided that such an investigation of a U.S. person is not conducted solely on the basis of First Amendment protected activities.

Finally, § 222 of the Communications Act of 1934, as amended, 47 U.S.C. § 222, restricts the voluntary disclosure of customer proprietary network information by telecommunications service providers. Violations of the pertinent provisions of law or regulation may expose service providers to criminal sanctions, civil penalties and forfeiture provisions, 47 U.S.C. §§ 501-503.[19]

Each of these statutory schemes is described in more detail below.

Pen Registers and Trap and Trace Devices for Foreign Intelligence and International Terrorism Investigations under FISA

Under 50 U.S.C. § 1842,[20] the Attorney General or a designated attorney for the government may apply for an ex parte court order authorizing the use of a pen register or trap and trace device to a Foreign Intelligence Surveillance Court (FISC) judge or to a U.S. magistrate judge designated by the Chief Justice of the United States to have the power to hear applications or grant orders approving installation and use of a pen register or trap and trace device on behalf of an FISC judge. The application must be approved by the Attorney General or a designated government attorney; must identify the federal officer seeking to use the pen register or trap and trace device; and must include a certification that the information likely to be obtained is foreign intelligence information[21] not concerning a U.S. person[22] or that the information is relevant to an ongoing investigation to protect against international terrorism or clandestine intelligence activities. An investigation of a U.S. person may not be conducted solely on the basis of First Amendment protected activities.

The order must specify the identity of the person who is the subject of the investigation, if known. If known, the order must identify the person to whom the telephone line or other facility to which the pen register or trap and trace device is to be attached is leased or in whose name it is listed. In addition, the order must list the attributes of the communications to which it applies, such as the number or other identifier and, if known, the location of the telephone line or other facility involved. In the case of a trap and trace device, the order must also identify the geographic limits of the trap and trace order.

Such an order, at the request of the applicant, also directs the provider of the wire or electronic service, landlord, custodian, or other person, to furnish any information, facilities, or technical assistance needed to accomplish the installation and operation of the pen register or trap and trace device in a manner that will protect its secrecy and minimize interference with the services provided. In addition, the order directs the provider, landlord, custodian, or other person not to disclose the existence of the investigation or the pen register or trap and trace device to anyone unless or until ordered to do so by the court. Records concerning the pen register or trap and trace device or the aid furnished are to be kept under security procedures approved by the Attorney General and the Director of National Security under 50 U.S.C. § 1805(b)(2)(C). The order also directs the applicant for the order to provide compensation for reasonable expenses incurred by the provider, landlord, custodian, or other person in providing information, facilities, or technical assistance.

Under 50 U.S.C. § 1842(d)(2)(C)(i), upon the request of the applicant for the court order, the court shall direct the wire or electronic service provider to provide the federal officer using the pen register or trap and trace device with the name; address; and the telephone number, instrument number or subscriber number or identifier of the customer or subscriber using the service covered by the order for the period specified by the order, including temporarily assigned network address or associated routing or transmission information. The service provider must also provide, if so ordered by the court upon the applicant's request, information on length of service of the customer or subscriber, as well as local or long distance telephone records of the subscriber or customer, and, if applicable, any records on periods of usage by the customer or subscriber. Further, the court, at the applicant's request, may order disclosure by the service provider of any mechanisms and sources of payment for the service (i.e., credit card, bank account).

Similarly, under 50 U.S.C. § 1842(d)(2)(C)(ii), if the information is available with respect to any customer or subscriber of incoming or outgoing communications to or from the service covered by the order, the court, upon the request of the applicant for the order, is to direct the wire or electronic service provider to provide the name; address; telephone number, instrument number or other subscriber number or identifier, of such customer or subscriber, as well as length of service provided to and types of serviced utilized by the subscriber or customer.

In general, the duration of an order issued under this section is not to exceed 90 days, with the possibility of extension for periods of not more than 90 days. However, if the applicant for the order certifies that the information likely to be obtained is foreign intelligence information not concerning a United States person, then an extension may be for up to a year. No cause of action may be brought against any wire or electronic service provider, landlord, custodian, or other person that furnishes information, facilities, or technical assistance pursuant to an order issued under this provision. Unless otherwise ordered by the judge, the results of the pen register or trap and trace device are to be provided to the authorized government official or officials at reasonable intervals.

Under 50 U.S.C. § 1805(i), as added by the FISA Amendments Act of 2008,[23] if an FISC judge grants an application by the government to conduct electronic surveillance under FISA, then, upon the request of the applicant, the FISC judge shall also authorize the installation and use of pen registers and trap and trace devices. In such circumstances, the provisions of 50 U.S.C. § 1842(d)(2) regarding disclosure of customer or subscriber information to the government would apply.

Pen Registers or Trap and Trace Devices Generally, and for Use in an Ongoing Criminal Investigation

18 U.S.C. § 3121 prohibits the installation and use of a pen register or trap and trace device without first obtaining a court order under FISA or under 18 U.S.C. § 3123. This prohibition does not apply to use by an electronic or wire service provider relating to:

- the operation, maintenance and testing of a service or protection of the rights or property of the service provider;
- the protection of users of the service from abuse or unlawful use of the service;
- to recording of the fact that a wire or electronic communication was initiated or completed to protect the service provider, another provider furnishing service toward completion of the wire communication, or a user of the service from fraudulent, unlawful or abusive use of the service; or
- to use where the consent of the user of the service has been obtained.

A government agency authorized to install and use a pen register or trap and trace device under the provisions of this chapter of Title 18, U.S.C., or under state law must use technology reasonably available to it that restricts the recording or decoding of electronic or other impulses to the dialing, routing, addressing, and signaling information utilized in the processing and transmitting of wire or electronic communications in a manner that does not include the contents of that communication.

An application for a court order authorizing a pen register or trap and trace device under this chapter must be made pursuant to 18 U.S.C. § 3122 in writing under oath or affirmation to a court of competent jurisdiction. Such an application must include the identity of the attorney for the government or the state law enforcement or investigative officer making the application and the identity of the law enforcement agency conducting the investigation, as well as a certification by the applicant that the information likely to be obtained is relevant to an ongoing criminal investigation being conducted by that agency.

Under 18 U.S.C. § 3123, the court shall enter an ex parte order authorization installation and use of a pen register or trap and trace device anywhere in the United States if the court finds that the applicant for the order has made such a certification. An order may authorize installation and use of a pen register or trap and trace device for a period of up to 60 days, which can be extended by court order for additional periods of no more than 60 days. The order must also direct that the order be sealed until otherwise ordered by the court, and must prohibit the person owning or leasing the line or other facility to which the pen register or trap and trace device is attached or applied, or who is obligated by the order to assist the applicant, from disclosing the existence of the pen register or trap and trace device or of the investigation to the listed subscriber or to any other person unless or until the court orders otherwise.[24]

Access to Business Records for Foreign Intelligence and International Terrorism Investigations

Under 50 U.S.C. § 1861, the Director of the Federal Bureau of Investigation (FBI) or a designee of the Director, whose rank shall not be lower than Assistant Special Agent in Charge, may apply to the FISA court for an order granting the government access to any tangible item (including books, records, papers, documents, and other items) for an investigation to obtain foreign intelligence information not concerning a United States person, or to protect against international terrorism or clandestine intelligence activities. Such an investigation of a United States person may not be conducted solely upon the basis of activities protected by the first amendment to the Constitution.

The application for such an order must include a statement of facts demonstrating that there are reasonable grounds to believe that the tangible things sought are relevant to an authorized or preliminary investigation to protect against international terrorism or espionage, or to obtain foreign intelligence information not concerning a U.S. person.[25] However, certain tangible items are deemed presumptively relevant to an investigation if the application's statement of facts shows that the items sought pertain to a foreign power or an agent of a foreign power, the activities of a suspected agent of a foreign power who is the subject of such authorized investigation, or an individual in contact with, or known to, a suspected agent of a foreign power who is the subject of such authorized investigation.[26]

The FISA court judge shall approve an application for an order under 50 U.S.C. § 1861, as requested or as modified, upon a finding that the application complies with statutory requirements. The order must contain a particularized description of the items sought, provide for a reasonable time to assemble them, and be limited to things which may be obtained under a grand jury subpoena or an order of a U.S. court for production of records or tangible things.[27] The order to produce the tangible things (production order) is also accompanied by a nondisclosure requirement (nondisclosure order) that prohibits the recipient from disclosing to any other person that the FBI has sought the tangible things described in the order, with limited exceptions.[28]

The recipient may immediately challenge the legality of the production order by filing a petition with the FISA court; however, the recipient must wait one year before challenging the nondisclosure order.[29] A FISA court judge considering the recipient's petition to modify or set aside the production order may do so only if the judge finds that the order does not meet statutory requirements or is otherwise unlawful.[30] A nondisclosure order may be modified or set aside if the judge finds that there is no reason to believe that disclosure may endanger the national security of the United States; interfere with a criminal, counterterrorism, or counterintelligence investigation; interfere with diplomatic relations; or endanger the life or physical safety of any person.[31] If, at the time the individual files the petition for judicial review of a nondisclosure order, the Attorney General, Deputy Attorney General, an Assistant Attorney General, or the Director of the FBI certifies that disclosure may endanger the national security of the United States or interfere with diplomatic relations, then the FISA judge must treat such government certification as conclusive unless the judge finds that the certification was made in bad faith.[32]

Authority to collect communications records under FISA is currently set to expire on December 31, 2009. After this date, and absent congressional extension, only records from common carriers, public accommodation facilities, storage facilities, and vehicle rental facilities may be sought under FISA.[33]

Access to Stored Electronic Communications and Transactional Records

Access to stored electronic communications and transactional records is addressed in 18 U.S.C. § 2701 *et seq.* Under 18 U.S.C. § 2702, voluntary disclosure of customer communications records by a service provider is prohibited unless it falls within one of several exceptions, including

- disclosure as authorized in 18 U.S.C. § 2703;
- disclosure with the lawful consent of the customer or subscriber; or
- disclosure to a governmental entity, if the provider, in good faith, believes that an emergency involving danger of death or serious physical injury to any person requires disclosure without delay of information relating to the emergency.[34]

In various reports regarding the use of "exigent letters," the DOJ OIG noted that one of the justifications for the use of exigent letters and other informal governmental requests for telephone records had been based upon this voluntary emergency disclosure provision.[35] However, these reports also concluded that many of the situations in which these tools were used did not appear to meet the emergency standard provided by this exception.[36]

Under 18 U.S.C. § 2703, a provider of electronic communication service or remote computing service shall disclose to a government entity the name, address, local and long distance telephone connection records, or records of session times and durations, length of service and types of service utilized, telephone instrument number or other subscriber number or identity, including temporarily assigned network address, and means and source of payment for such service pursuant to

- a warrant;
- a court order based upon specific and articulable facts showing that there are reasonable grounds to believe that the contents of a wire or electronic communication or the records or other information sought are relevant and material to an ongoing criminal investigation;

- customer or subscriber consent;
- a written request from the governmental entity relevant to a law enforcement investigation regarding telemarketing fraud;
- an administrative subpoena authorized by federal or state statute, or
- a federal or state grand jury subpoena or trial subpoena.

A governmental entity receiving such records or information is not required to provide notice to a subscriber or customer. Nor does any cause of action lie against any service provider of wire or electronic communication service, its officers, employees, agents, or other specified persons for providing information, facilities, or assistance in accordance with the terms of a court order, warrant, subpoena, statutory authorization or certification under this chapter.

18 U.S.C. § 2706 requires a government entity obtaining records or other information under §§ 2702 or 2703 to reimburse the costs reasonably necessary and directly incurred in searching for, assembling, reproducing or otherwise providing such information. The amount of payment is to be mutually agreed upon by the government entity and the person or entity providing the information, or, in the absence of an agreement, determined by the court issuing the production order. The reimbursement requirement does not apply to records or other information maintained by a communications common carrier that relate to telephone records and telephone listings obtained under 18 U.S.C. § 2703 unless a court orders payment upon a determination that the information required is unusually voluminous in nature or otherwise caused an undue burden upon the provider.

National Security Letters

Under 18 U.S.C. § 2709, a national security letter provision,[37] wire or electronic service providers[38] must provide subscriber information and toll billing records information, or electronic communication transactional records in its custody or possession in response to a request by the Director of the Federal Bureau of Investigation (FBI) if the Director of the FBI, or his designee in a position not lower than Deputy Assistant Director at Bureau headquarters or a Special Agent in Charge designated by the FBI Director in a field office, certifies that the records or information sought is relevant to an authorized investigation to protect against international terrorism or clandestine intelligence activities, provided that such an investigation of a U.S. person is not conducted solely on the basis of First Amendment protected activities.

Under 18 U.S.C. § 2709(b), if the Director of the Federal Bureau of Investigation, or his designee, certifies that disclosure of the request may result in a danger to the national security of the United States, interference with a criminal, counterterrorism, or counterintelligence investigation, interference with diplomatic relations, or danger to the life or physical safety of any person, no wire or electronic communications service provider, or officer, employee, or agent thereof, shall disclose to any person (other than those to whom such disclosure is necessary to comply with the request or an attorney to obtain legal advice or legal assistance with respect to the request) that the Federal Bureau of Investigation has sought or obtained access to information or records under this section.[39] The FBI must notify the person or entity to whom a §2709(b) request is made where such a nondisclosure requirement is applicable. A recipient of such a request who notifies those to whom notice is necessary for compliance with the request or who notifies an attorney to obtain legal advice or legal assistance with respect to the request must also advise them of the nondisclosure requirement.

At the request of the Director of the Federal Bureau of Investigation or the designee of the Director, any person making or intending to make a disclosure under this section shall identify to the Director or such designee the person to whom such disclosure will be made or to whom such disclosure was made prior to the request, except that nothing in this section shall require a person to inform the Director or such designee of the identity of an attorney to whom disclosure was made or will be made to obtain legal advice or legal assistance with respect to the request.

The FBI may only disseminate records obtained under this section as provided in guidelines approved by the Attorney General for foreign intelligence collection and foreign counterintelligence investigations conducted by the Federal Bureau of Investigation, and, with respect to dissemination to an agency of the United States, only if such information is clearly relevant to the authorized responsibilities of such agency. On a semiannual basis, the Director of the Federal Bureau of Investigation is required to fully inform the Permanent Select Committee on Intelligence of the House of Representatives and the Select Committee on Intelligence of the Senate, and the Committee on the Judiciary of the House of Representatives and the Committee on the Judiciary of the Senate, concerning all requests made under subsection (b) of this section.

Penalties

Except as provided in 18 U.S.C. § 2703(e), 18 U.S.C. § 2707 provides a civil cause of action for any provider of electronic communication service, subscriber, or other person aggrieved by a knowing or intentional violation of this chapter. The aggrieved party may receive equitable relief and damages. The damages which may be assessed by the court are actual damages suffered by the plaintiff plus any profits made by the violator as a result of the violation. At a minimum, a person entitled to recover damages must receive no less than $1,000. If a court or appropriate department or agency determines that the United States has violated this chapter and that the circumstances surrounding the violation raise questions as to whether a federal officer or employee acted willfully or intentionally with respect to the violation, disciplinary action against that officer or employee may also be initiated.

A person aggrieved by a willful violation of this chapter or a willful violation of 50 U.S.C. § 1845(a), which deals with the use of information gathered through a pen register and trap and trace under FISA, may commence a civil action against the United States in a U.S. district court to receive money damages under 18 U.S.C. § 2712. If the claim is successful in establishing such a violation, the court may assess actual damages, but not less than $10,000, whichever is greater, plus reasonably incurred litigation costs. There is a two year statute of limitations applicable to this provision, and this section states that this is the exclusive remedy against the United States for claims within the purview of the section. The agency or department must reimburse any award under this section to the U.S. treasury. Administrative discipline may also be pursued. A proceeding under 18 U.S.C. § 2712 shall be stayed by the court, upon motion by the United States, if the court determines that civil discovery will adversely affect the government's ability to conduct a related investigation or prosecution of a related criminal case. Such a stay also tolls the statute of limitations.

Communications Act of 1934

Telecommunications carriers are also subject to obligations to guard the confidentiality of customer proprietary network information (CPNI) and to ensure that it is not disclosed to third parties without customer approval or as required by law. Section 222 of the Communication Act of 1934, as amended, establishes a duty of every telecommunications carrier to protect the confidentiality of its customers' customer proprietary network information.[40]

Section 222 attempts to achieve a balance between marketing and customer privacy.

CPNI includes personally identifiable information derived from a customer's relationship with a telephone company, irrespective of whether the customer purchases landline or wireless telephone service. CPNI is defined as

> (A) information that relates to the quantity, technical configuration, type, destination, location, and amount of use of a telecommunications service subscribed to by any customer of a telecommunications carrier, and that is made available to the carrier by the customer solely by virtue of the carrier-customer relationship; and (B) information contained in the bills pertaining to telephone exchange service or telephone toll service received by a customer of a carrier.[41]

CPNI includes customers' calling activities and history (e.g., phone numbers called, frequency, duration, and time), and billing records.[42] It does not include subscriber list information, such as name, address, and phone number.[43]

In section 222, Congress created a framework to govern telecommunications carriers' use of information obtained through provision of a telecommunications service. Section 222 of the act provides that telecommunications carriers must protect the confidentiality of customer proprietary network information. The act limits carriers' abilities to use customer phone records, including for their own marketing purposes, without customer approval and appropriate safeguards. The act also prohibits carriers from using, disclosing, or permitting access to this information without the approval of the customer, or as otherwise required by law, if the use or disclosure is not in connection with the provided service.

Section 222(a) imposes a general duty on telecommunications carriers to protect the confidentiality of proprietary information of other carriers, equipment manufacturers, and customers.[44] Section 222(b) states that a carrier that receives or obtains proprietary information from other carriers in order to provide a telecommunications service may use such information only for that purpose and may not use that information for its own marketing efforts.[45]

The confidentiality protections applicable to customer proprietary network information are established in section 222(c). Subsection (c)(1) constitutes the core privacy requirement for telecommunications carriers.

> Except as required by law or with the approval of the customer, a telecommunications carrier that receives or obtains customer proprietary

> network information by virtue of its provision of a telecommunications service shall only use, disclose, or permit access to individually identifiable customer proprietary network information in its provision of (A) the telecommunications service from which such information is derived, or (B) services necessary to, or used in, the provision of such telecommunications service, including the publishing of directories.[46]

Section 222(c)(2) provides that a carrier must disclose CPNI "upon affirmative written request by the customer, to any person designated by the customer."[47] Section 222(c)(3) provides that a carrier may use, disclose, or permit access to aggregate customer information other than for the purposes described in subsection (1).[48] Thus, the general principle of confidentiality for customer information is that a carrier may only use, disclose, or permit access to customers' individually identifiable CPNI in limited circumstances: (1) as required by law;[49] (2) with the customer's approval; or (3) in its provision of the telecommunications service from which such information is derived, or services necessary to or used in the provision of such telecommunications service.

Exceptions to the general principle of confidentiality permit carriers to use, disclose, or permit access to customer proprietary network information to (1) initiate, render, bill, and collect for telecommunications services; (2) protect the rights or property of the carrier, the customers, and other carriers from fraudulent, abusive, or unlawful use of, or subscription to, such services; (3) provide any inbound telemarketing, referral, or administrative services to the customer for the duration of the call; and (4) provide call location information concerning the user of a commercial mobile service for emergency.[50]

Section 222(e) addresses the disclosure of subscriber list information, and permits carriers to provide subscriber list information to any person upon request for the purpose of publishing directories. The term "subscriber list information" means any information identifying the listed names of subscribers of a carrier and such subscribers' telephone numbers, addresses, or primary advertising classifications, or any combination of such listed names, numbers, addresses, or classifications; that the carrier or an affiliate has published, caused to be published, or accepted for publication in any directory format.[51]

Customer Proprietary Network Information (CPNI) Regulations

In 1998, the Federal Communications Commission issued its *CPNI Order* to implement section 222.[52] The *CPNI Order* and subsequent orders issued by the Commission govern the use and disclosure of customer proprietary network information by telecommunications carriers. When the FCC implemented Section 222, telecommunications carriers were required to obtain express consent from their customers (i.e., "opt-in consent") before a carrier could use customer phone records to market services outside of the customer's relationship with the carrier. The United States Court of Appeals for the Tenth Circuit struck down those rules, finding that they violated the First and Fifth Amendments of the Constitution.[53]

Subsequently, the FCC amended its CPNI regulations to require telecommunications carriers to receive opt-in (affirmative) consent before disclosing CPNI to third parties or affiliates that do not provide communications-related services.[54] However, carriers are permitted to disclose CPNI to affiliated parties after obtaining a customer's "opt-out" consent.[55] "Opt-Out" consent means that the telephone company sends the customer a notice saying it will consider the customer to have given approval to use the customer's information for marketing unless the customer tells it not to do so (usually within 30 days.)[56] Carriers are required, prior to soliciting the customer's approval, to provide notice to the customer of the customer's right to restrict use, disclosure, and access to the customer's CPNI.[57] Carriers are also required to establish safeguards to protect against the unauthorized disclosure of CPNI, including requirements that carriers maintain records that track access to customer CPNI records.[58] Each carrier is also required to certify annually its compliance with the CPNI requirements and to make this certification publicly available.[59] The FCC recently proposed $100,000 fines on telephone companies with inadequate certifications regarding compliance with FCC rules protecting customer information from disclosure.[60] A suit challenging the opt-in requirement is currently pending before the D.C. Circuit.[61]

Penalties

Carriers in violation of the CPNI requirements are subject to a variety of penalties under the act. Under the criminal penalty provision in section 501 of the act, 47 U.S.C. § 501, any person who willfully and knowingly does, causes or allows to be done, any act, matter, or thing prohibited by the act or declared unlawful, or who willfully and knowingly omits or fails to do what is required by the act, or who willfully or knowingly causes or allows such omission or failure, shall be punished for any such offense for which no penalty (other than a forfeiture) is provided by the act by a fine up to $10,000, imprisonment up to one year, or both, and in the case of a person previously convicted of violating the act, a fine up to $10,000, imprisonment up to two years, or both.

Section 502 of the act, 47 U.S.C. § 502, punishes willful and knowing violations of Federal Communication Commission regulations. Any person who willfully and knowingly violates any rule, regulation, restriction, or condition made or imposed by the Commission is, in addition to other penalties provided by law, subject to a maximum fine of $500 for each day on which a violation occurs.[62]

Under section 503(b)(1) of the act, 47 U.S.C. § 503(b)(1), any person who is determined by the Commission to have willfully or repeatedly failed to comply with any provision of the act or any rule, regulation, or order issued by the Commission shall be liable to the United States for a civil money "forfeiture" penalty.[63] Section 312(f)(1) of the act, 47 U.S.C. § 312(f)(1), defines "willful" as "the conscious and deliberate commission or omission of [any] act, irrespective of any intent to violate" the law. "Repeated" means that the act was committed or omitted more than once, or lasts more than one day. If the violator is a common carrier, section 503(b) authorizes the Commission to assess a forfeiture penalty of up to $130,000 for each violation or for each day of a continuing violation, except that the amount assessed for any continuing violation shall not exceed a total of $1,325,000 for any single act or failure to act.[64] To impose such a forfeiture penalty, the Commission must issue a notice of apparent liability, and the person against whom the notice has been issued must have an opportunity to show, in writing, why no such forfeiture penalty should be imposed. The Commission will then issue a forfeiture if it finds by a preponderance of the evidence that the person has violated the act or a Commission rule.

End Notes

[1] Leslie Cauley, *NSA Has Massive Database of Americans' Phone Calls; 3 Telecoms Help Government Collect Billions of Domestic Records*, USA TODAY, May 11, 2006, at 1A. The story alleged that Verizon, BellSouth, and AT&T provided calling records in response to the NSA's inquiry or production demand, while Qwest did not. In December of 2008, more revelations regarding an alleged NSA program, given the codename "Stellar Wind," were reported in the December 22, 2008, issue of *Newsweek*. *See* Michael Isikoff, *The Fed Who Blew the Whistle*, NEWSWEEK, Dec. 22, 2008, at 40, 44.

[2] U.S. DEPARTMENT OF JUSTICE, OFFICE OF THE INSPECTOR GENERAL, *A Review of the Federal Bureau of Investigation's Use of Exigent Letters and Other Informal Requests for*

Telephone Records (Jan. 2010), available at http://www.justice.gov/oig/special/s1001r.pdf; U.S. DEPARTMENT OF JUSTICE, OFFICE OF THE INSPECTOR GENERAL, *A Review of the Federal Bureau of Investigation's Use of National Security Letters*, at 96 (March 2007), available at http://www.usdoj.gov/oig/special/s0703b/final.pdf.

[3] *Id.* at 92-93.

[4] A pen register is a device or process which records the dialing, routing, addressing, or signaling information transmitted in conjunction with an electronic communication, but does not record the contents of that communication. *See* 18 U.S.C. § 3127(3).

[5] U.S. CONST. amend. IV.

[6] 442 U.S. 735 (1979).

[7] 389 U.S. 347 (1967).

[8] *Smith*, 442 U.S. at 741 (emphasis in original).

[9] *Id.* at 742 (quoting United States v. New York Tel. Co., 434 U.S. 159, 174-75 (1977)).

[10] *Id.* at 744.

[11] *Id.* at 745-46.

[12] *Id.* at 747-48 (Stewart, J., dissenting).

[13] *Id.* at 749 (Marshall, J., dissenting).

[14] Under 50 U.S.C. § 1841(2), which cross references the definition in 18 U.S.C. § 3127(3), the term "pen register" "means a device or process which records or decodes dialing, routing, addressing, or signaling information transmitted by an instrument or facility from which a wire or electronic communication is transmitted, provided, however, that such information shall not include the contents of any communication, but such term does not include any device or process used by a provider or customer of a wire or electronic communication service for billing, or recording as an incident to billing, for communications services provided by such provider or any device or process used by a provider or customer of a wire communication service for cost accounting or other like purposes in the ordinary course of its business."

[15] Under 50 U.S.C. § 1841(2), which cross references the definition in 18 U.S.C. § 3127(4), the term "trap and trace device" "means a device or process which captures the incoming electronic or other impulses which identify the originating number or other dialing, routing, addressing, and signaling information reasonably likely to identify the source of a wire or electronic communication, provided, however, that such information shall not include the contents of any communication."

[16] Under 50 U.S.C. § 1861, an investigation concerning a U.S. person may not be based solely on First Amendment protected activities.

[17] *See* CRS Report RL33320, *National Security Letters in Foreign Intelligence Investigations: Legal Background and Recent Amendments*, by Charles Doyle.

[18] Under 18 U.S.C. § 2709(f), "A library (as that term is defined in section 213(1) of the Library Services and Technology Act (20 U.S.C. 9122(1)), the services of which include access to the Internet, books, journals, magazines, newspapers, or other similar forms of communication in print or digitally by patrons for their use, review, examination, or circulation, is not a wire or electronic communication service provider for purposes of this section, unless the library is providing the services defined in section 2510(15) ("electronic communication service") of this title." Subsection (f) was added by P.L. 109-178, § 5.

[19] *See* CRS Report RL34409, *Selected Laws Governing the Disclosure of Customer Phone Records by Telecommunications Carriers*, by Kathleen Ann Ruane.

[20] Other provisions of this chapter deal with authorization for pen registers or trap and trace devices during emergencies, 50 U.S.C. § 1843, authorization during time of war, 50 U.S.C. 1844, use of information gathered under a FISA pen register or trap and trace device, 50 U.S.C. § 1845, and congressional oversight, 50 U.S.C. § 1846.

[21] Under 18 U.S.C. § 1801(e), "foreign intelligence information" is defined to mean information that relates to, and if concerning a United States person is necessary to, the ability of the United States to protect against actual or potential attack or other grave hostile acts of a

foreign power or an agent of a foreign power, sabotage or international terrorism by a foreign power or an agent of a foreign power, or clandestine intelligence activities by an intelligence service or network of a foreign power or by an agent of a foreign power; or information with respect to a foreign power or foreign territory that relates to, and if concerning a United States person is necessary to the national defense or the security of the United States or the conduct of the foreign affairs of the United States. The phrase "agents of a foreign power" currently includes, among others, non-U.S. persons that are engaged in international terrorism, but are not linked to an identifiable terrorist organization or foreign government. For a more detailed discussion of treatment of so-called "lone wolf" terrorists under FISA, *see* CRS Report R40138, *Amendments to the Foreign Intelligence Surveillance Act (FISA) Set to Expire February 28, 2010*, by Anna C. Henning and Edward C. Liu, at 2-4.

[22] Under 50 U.S.C. § 1801(i), "United States person" means a citizen of the United States, an alien lawfully admitted for permanent residence (as defined in section 1101(a)(20) of Title 8), an unincorporated association a substantial number of members of which are citizens of the United States or aliens lawfully admitted for permanent residence, or a corporation which is incorporated in the United States, but does not include a corporation or an association which is a foreign power, as defined in subsection (a)(1), (2), or (3) of this section.

[23] P.L. 110-261, § 105.

[24] 18 U.S.C. § 3124 addresses assistance in installation and use of the pen register or trap and trace device; while 18 U.S.C. § 3125 deals with emergency installation of a pen register and trap or trap and trace device. 18 U.S.C. § 2136 provides for annual reports to Congress by the Attorney General on the number of applications by law enforcement agencies of the Department of Justice for pen registers or trap and trace devices orders, as well as certain details with respect to court orders issued in response to such applications.

[25] 50 U.S.C. § 1861(b)(2)(A).

[26] The phrase "agents of a foreign power" currently includes, among others, non-U.S. persons that are engaged in international terrorism, but are not linked to an identifiable terrorist organization or foreign government. For a more detailed discussion of treatment of so-called "lone wolf" terrorists under FISA, *see* CRS Report R40138, *Amendments to the Foreign Intelligence Surveillance Act (FISA) Set to Expire February 28, 2010*, by Anna C. Henning and Edward C. Liu, at 2-4.

[27] 50 U.S.C. § 1861(c).

[28] A recipient of a FISA order under this section may disclose its existence to persons to whom disclosure is necessary to comply with the order, to an attorney to obtain legal advice with respect to the production of things in response to the order, as well as to other persons approved by the FBI. 50 U.S.C. § 1861(d)(1).

[29] 50 U.S.C. § 1861(f)(2)(A).

[30] 50 U.S.C. § 1861(f)(2)(B).

[31] 50 U.S.C. § 1861(f)(2)(C)(i).

[32] 50 U.S.C. § 1861(f)(2)(C)(ii).

[33] *See* CRS Report R40138, *Amendments to the Foreign Intelligence Surveillance Act (FISA) Set to Expire February 28, 2010*, by Anna C. Henning and Edward C. Liu, at 7-11.

[34] This language was added by P.L. 109-177, Title I, § 107(b)(1)(B). It replaced an exception which covered "disclosure to a governmental entity if the provider reasonably believes that an emergency involving immediate danger of death or serious physical injury to any person justifies disclosure of the information."

[35] U.S. DEPARTMENT OF JUSTICE OFFICE OF THE INSPECTOR GENERAL, *A Review of the Federal Bureau of Investigation's Use of Exigent Letters and Other Informal Requests for Telephone Records*, at 260-263, 269 (Jan. 2010), available at http://www.justice.. gov/oig/special/s1001r.pdf; U.S. DEPARTMENT OF JUSTICE OFFICE OF THE INSPECTOR

GENERAL, *Review of the Federal Bureau of Investigation's Use of National Security Letters*, at 96 (March 2007), available at http://www.usdoj.gov/oig/special/s0703b/final.pdf.

[36] *Id.*

[37] *See* CRS Report RL33320, *National Security Letters in Foreign Intelligence Investigations: Legal Background and Recent Amendments*, by Charles Doyle.

[38] Under 18 U.S.C. § 2709(f), "A library (as that term is defined in section 213(1) of the Library Services and Technology Act (20 U.S.C. 9122(1)), the services of which include access to the Internet, books, journals, magazines, newspapers, or other similar forms of communication in print or digitally by patrons for their use, review, examination, or circulation, is not a wire or electronic communication service provider for purposes of this section, unless the library is providing the services defined in section 2510(15) ("electronic communication service") of this title." Subsection (f) was added by P.L. 109-178, § 5.

[39] P.L. 109-177, § 116(a), rewrote subsection (c) of 18 U.S.C. § 2709, which formerly read, "No wire or electronic communication service provider, or officer, employee, or agent thereof, shall disclose to any person that the Federal Bureau of Investigation has sought or obtained access to information or records under this section." P.L. 109-178, § 4(b), rewrote subsection (c)(4), as amended by P.L. 109-177, § 116(a), which formerly read, "At the request of the Director of the Federal Bureau of Investigation or the designee of the Director, any person making or intending to make a disclosure under this section shall identify to the Director or such designee the person to whom such disclosure will be made or to whom such disclosure was made prior to the request, but in no circumstance shall a person be required to inform the Director or such designee that the person intends to consult an attorney to obtain legal advice or legal assistance."

[40] 47 U.S.C. § 222. Section 222 was added to the Communications Act by the Telecommunications Act of 1996. Telecommunications Act of 1996, P.L. 104-104, 110 Stat. 56 (codified at 47 U.S.C. §§ 151 et seq.).

[41] 47 U.S.C. § 222(h)(1).

[42] *See* FED. COMM. COMM'N, *Protecting Your Telephone Calling Records* (Oct. 20, 2008) available at http://www.fcc.gov/cgb/consumerfacts/phoneaboutyou.html.

[43] 47 U.S.C. § 222(h)(3).

[44] 47 U.S.C.§ 222(a).

[45] 47 U.S.C. § 222(b).

[46] 47 U.S.C. § 222(c)(1).

[47] 47 U.S.C. § 222(c)(2).

[48] 47 U.S.C. § 222(c)(3). The term "aggregate customer information" means collective data that relates to a group or category of services or customers, from which individual customer identities and characteristics have been removed. 47 U.S.C. § 222(h)(2).

[49] Whether the statutory provisions discussed in this report would fall within this exception is uncertain.

[50] 47 U.S.C. § 222(d).

[51] 47 U.S.C. § 222(e).

[52] *CPNI Order*, 13 FCC Rcd 8061.

[53] *U.S. West v. FCC*, 182 F.3d 1224 (10th Cir. 1999), *cert. denied Competition Policy Instit. v. U.S. West, Inc.*, 530 U.S. 1213 (2000).

[54] Except as required by law, carriers may not disclose CPNI to third parties or their own affiliates that do not provide communications-related services unless the consumer has given "opt in" consent, which is express written, oral, or electronic consent. 47 C.F.R. §§ 64.2005(b), 64.2007(b)(3); 64.2008(e); see also 47 C.F.R. § 64.2003(h) (defining "opt-in approval").

[55] 47 C.F.R. §§ 64.2005(b), 64.2007(b)(1).

[56] FCC Consumer Advisory: Protecting the Privacy of Your Telephone Calling Records, at http://www.fcc.gov/cgb/ consumerfacts/phoneaboutyou.html.

[57] 47 C.F.R. §§ 64.2008.

[58] 47 C.F.R. §§ 64.2009.

[59] 47 C.F.R. §§ 64.2009(e).

[60] In the Matter of Cbeyond Communications, LLC, 2006 FCC LEXIS 1902 (April 21, 2006), at http://www.fcc.gov/ eb/Orders/2006/DA-06-916A1.html.

[61] *See* CRS Report RL34409, *Selected Laws Governing the Disclosure of Customer Phone Records by Telecommunications Carriers*, by Kathleen Ann Ruane, at 9.

[62] 47 U.S.C. § 502.

[63] 47 U.S.C. § 503(b)(1).

[64] FCC Forfeiture Proceedings, Limits on the amount of forfeiture assessed, 47 C.F.R. Part 1.80(b).

In: Government Access and Collection of Private... ISBN: 978-1-60876-085-5
Editors: Corey D. Heims

Chapter 2

GOVERNMENT COLLECTION OF PRIVATE INFORMATION: BACKGROUND AND ISSUES RELATED TO THE USA PATRIOT ACT REAUTHORIZATION

Anna C. Henning, Elizabeth B. Bazan, Charles Doyle and Edward C. Liu

SUMMARY

Congress enacted the USA PATRIOT Act soon after the 9/11 terrorist attacks. The most controversial sections of the act facilitate the federal government's collection of more information, from a greater number of sources, than had previously been authorized in criminal or foreign intelligence investigations. The Foreign Intelligence Surveillance Act (FISA), the Electronic Communications Privacy Act (ECPA), and the national security letter (NSL) statutes were all bolstered. With the changes came greater access to records showing an individual's spending and communication patterns as well as increased authority to intercept e-mail and telephone conversations and to search homes and businesses. In some cases, evidentiary standards required to obtain court approval for the collection of information were lowered. Other approaches included expanding the scope of information subject to search, adding flexibility to the methods by which information could be collected, and broadening the purposes for which information may be sought.

Some perceived the changes as necessary to unearth terrorist cells and update investigative authorities to respond to the new technologies and characteristics of ever-shifting threats. Others argued that authorities granted by the USA PATRIOT Act and subsequent measures could unnecessarily undermine constitutional rights over time. In response to such concerns, sunset provisions were established for many of the changes.

Subsequent measures made most of the USA PATRIOT Act changes permanent. However, three authorities affecting the collection of foreign intelligence information are set to expire on February 28, 2011: the lone wolf, roving wiretap, and business record sections of FISA. The 111th Congress replaced an earlier expiration date with the 2011 date. Before that change was made, the impending expiration prompted legislative proposals which revisit changes made by the USA PATRIOT Act and related measures. Two such bills—the USA PATRIOT Act Sunset Extension Act of 2009 (S. 1692) and the USA PATRIOT Amendments Act of 2009 (H.R. 3845)—were reported from their respective judiciary committees.

In addition to the expiring provisions, these and other bills introduced during the 111th Congress (e.g., S. 1686, S. 1725, S. 1726, S. 2336, H.R. 1800, H.R. 3846, H.R. 3969, and H.R. 4005) address a range of issues, including national security letters, minimization requirements, nondisclosure requirements (gag orders), interception of international communications, and retroactive repeal of communication provider immunity for Terrorist Surveillance Program (TSP) assistance. This report surveys the legal environment in which the legislative proposals arise.

Introduction

Shortly after the 9/11 terrorist attacks, Congress enacted the USA PATRIOT Act, in part, to "provid[e] enhanced investigative tools" to "assist in the prevention of future terrorist activities and the preliminary acts and crimes which further such activities."[1] To that end, the act eased restrictions on the government's ability to collect information regarding people's activities and conversations, both in domestic criminal investigations and in the realms of foreign intelligence gathering and national security. The changes are perceived by many to be necessary in light of the new breed of threats in a post-9/11 world.[2] The expanded authorities also prompted concerns regarding the appropriate balance between national security interests and civil liberties.[3] In part for that reason, the changes were revisited and modified in subsequent measures.[4]

Several bills introduced during the 111th Congress propose further adjustments to USA PATRIOT Act provisions and related authorities for the government's collection of private information. Two relevant bills—the USA PATRIOT Act Sunset Extension Act of 2009 (S. 1692) and the USA PATRIOT Amendments Act of 2009 (H.R. 3845)—were reported from their respective judiciary committees.[5]

These and other legislative proposals were catalyzed, in part, by a sunset date (originally December 31, 2009) for three amendments which expanded authorities for the collection of foreign intelligence information.[6] The sunset date is now February 28, 2011.[7] However, bills introduced during the 111th Congress cover a range of authorities expanded by the USA PATRIOT Act in addition to the expiring provisions.

This report discusses the history of constitutional interpretations and legislative responses relevant to the collection of private information for criminal investigation, foreign intelligence gathering, and national security purposes. Next, it summarizes the relevant statutory frameworks and changes made by the USA PATRIOT Act and subsequent measures. It then examines congressional oversight, judicial review, and "minimization procedures" designed to limit the extent of government intrusions where possible. Finally, it discusses several related matters likely to play a role in the legislative debate surrounding reauthorization of the expiring provisions.

CONSTITUTIONAL LIMITATIONS

Constitutional limitations restrict the government's ability to access private information. The Fourth Amendment to the U.S. Constitution is particularly relevant. To the extent that government activity burdens individuals' freedom of speech and related rights, the First Amendment may also play a role.

Fourth Amendment

The Fourth Amendment to the U.S. Constitution provides a right "of the people to be secure in their persons, houses, papers, and effects, against unreasonable searches and seizures."[8] Many of the government activities discussed in this report have the potential to constitute a search as that term is defined in Fourth Amendment jurisprudence. Namely, government action constitutes a search when it intrudes upon a person's "reasonable expectation of privacy," which requires both that an "individual manifested a subjective expectation of privacy in the searched object" and that "society is willing to recognize that expectation as reasonable."[9]

Thus, the Fourth Amendment ultimately limits the government's ability to conduct a range of activities, such as physical searches of homes or offices and listening to phone conversations. As a general rule, the Fourth Amendment requires the government to demonstrate "probable cause" and obtain a warrant (unless a recognized warrant exception applies) before conducting a search.[10] This rule applies most clearly in criminal investigations. For example, an officer conducting a criminal investigation typically may not search a person's belongings without first obtaining a warrant that describes the property for which sufficient evidence justifies a search.

The extent to which the Fourth Amendment warrant requirement applies to the government's collection of information for intelligence gathering and other purposes unrelated to criminal investigations is unclear. Although the surveillance of wire or oral communications for criminal law enforcement purposes was held to be subject to the warrant requirement of the Fourth Amendment in 1967,[11] neither the Supreme Court nor Congress sought to regulate the use of such surveillance for national security purposes at that time. Several years later, the Supreme Court invalidated warrantless electronic surveillance of domestic organizations for national security purposes, but indicated that its conclusion might differ if the electronic surveillance targeted foreign powers or their agents.[12] A lower court has since upheld the statutory scheme governing the gathering of foreign intelligence information against a Fourth Amendment challenge, despite an assumption that orders issued pursuant to the statute might not constitute "warrants" for Fourth Amendment purposes.[13] The Supreme Court has not yet directly addressed the issue. However, even if the warrant requirement was found not to apply to searches for foreign intelligence or national security purposes, such searches would presumably be subject to the general Fourth Amendment "reasonableness" test.[14]

In contrast with its rulings on surveillance, the Supreme Court has not historically applied the protections of the Fourth Amendment to documents held by third parties. In 1976, it held that financial records in the possession of third parties could be obtained by the government without a warrant.[15] Later, it likewise held that the installation and use of a pen register—a device used to capture telephone numbers dialed—does not constitute a Fourth Amendment search.[16] The reasoning was that individuals have a lesser expectation of privacy with regard to information held by third parties.

First Amendment

The First Amendment to the U.S. Constitution restricts government efforts to prohibit the free exercise of religion or to abridge free speech, freedom of the press, the right to peaceful assembly, or the right to petition for redress of grievances.[17] Two First Amendment concerns arise with regard to electronic surveillance, access to records, and related investigatory activities. One addresses direct restrictions on speech that may accompany government collection of private information, such as non-disclosure requirements accompanying orders compelling government access to business records, discussed *infra*. A second concern is that overly broad authorities permitting government intrusion may lead to a "chilling" (i.e., stifling) effect on public discourse.[18] Some post-9/11 laws address the latter issue directly, for example by prohibiting investigations based solely on a person's First Amendment activities.[19] Despite safeguards, there is concern that post-9/11 authorities may have been used to circumvent First Amendment limitations on analogous authorities.[20]

History of Congressional Action

Congress addressed the federal government's access to private information following key Supreme Court decisions interpreting the Fourth Amendment. In 1968, it enacted legislation, Title III of the Omnibus Crime Control and Safe Streets Act, which outlawed the unauthorized interception of wire or oral communications and authorized interception under court supervision for law enforcement purposes.[21] Later, it passed the Electronic

Communications Privacy Act (ECPA), which incorporated and modernized Title III to cover electronic as well as wire and oral communications.[22]

In the years following the Supreme Court's 1972 ruling on surveillance (the "*Keith* case"), Congress actively examined the intelligence practices of past presidential administrations and found that every administration since Franklin D. Roosevelt engaged in electronic surveillance without prior judicial approval.[23] It also found that the authority was sometimes abused.[24] Partly in light of these findings, Congress enacted the Foreign Intelligence Surveillance Act (FISA)[25] to create a statutory framework for the use of electronic surveillance to collect foreign intelligence information.

Similarly, in response to the Supreme Court's rulings regarding the Fourth Amendment's non-application to documents held by third parties, Congress enacted the Right to Financial Privacy Act (RFPA)[26] to constrain government authorities' access to individuals' financial records. Although these privacy protections are subject to a foreign intelligence exception,[27] government authorities were not authorized to compel financial institutions to secretly turn over financial records until 1986.[28] That year, the FBI was also given authority, in the form of FBI-issued "national security letters," to access customer records held by telephone companies and other communications service providers in specified instances justified by a national security rationale.[29] Two additional national security letter authorities were enacted in the mid-1990s. The first provided access to credit and financial records of federal employees with security clearances.[30] The second gave the FBI access to credit agency records in order to facilitate the identification of financial institutions utilized by the target of an investigation.[31]

Intelligence gathering laws were expanded during the same time period. In 1994, FISA was amended to cover physical searches for foreign intelligence purposes.[32] Four years later, Congress amended FISA to permit the Foreign Intelligence Surveillance Court to issue orders authorizing (1) the use of pen registers and trap and trace devices to track calling patterns;[33] and (2) the production of some business records not available through existing national security letter authorities.[34]

The USA PATRIOT Act,[35] enacted in 2001, represented a broad expansion of existing statutory authorities. It eliminated barriers to cooperation between law enforcement and foreign intelligence investigations, modified surveillance authorities under both FISA and ECPA, and created a fifth category of national security letters. Many of these provisions were made temporary, subject to sunset in 2005.[36]

In 2004, Congress enacted the Intelligence Reform and Terrorism Prevention Act. Among other things, the act amended FISA to allow targeting so-called "lone wolves" or individuals believed to be engaged in terrorism, but who were not linked to a known terrorist organization.[37] The "lone wolf" provision was given an expiration date to match that which applied to many of the USA PATRIOT Act provisions.

The next year, Congress reauthorized the USA PATRIOT Act, making the majority of its expiring provisions permanent.[38] However, two of its most controversial provisions, discussed *infra*, together with the 2004 lone wolf provision, were given a new sunset date of December 31, 2009.[39]

Also in 2005, President Bush acknowledged that he had authorized a Terrorist Surveillance Program (TSP), which captured some international communications apparently procured without judicial or statutory authority. As discussed *infra*, Congress subsequently enacted the Protect America Act and the FISA Amendments Act of 2008, which addressed issues raised in response to the TSP.

In December 2009 and again in February 2010, Congress temporarily extended the sunset date for the lone wolf and two USA PATRIOT Act provisions which were scheduled to sunset in 2009.[40] They are now set to expire on February 28, 2011.

Statutory Framework

The applicable statutory regime or procedural rules differ according to the purpose for which the federal government collects private information. In criminal law enforcement investigations, the Federal Rules of Criminal Procedure, ECPA, and other provisions in Title 18 of the U.S. Code apply. In contrast, the collection of foreign intelligence information is governed by FISA. Finally, five national security statutes, discussed *infra*, regulate the issuance of national security letters. Statutes in these areas provide analogous authorities for various government activities but require that different standards and procedures be satisfied.

Federal Rules of Criminal Procedure and Subpoena Authorities

In criminal cases, federal officials ordinarily gain access to spaces, documents, and other private materials pursuant to a warrant (during investigation) or a subpoena (during prosecution). In criminal investigations, Federal Rule of Criminal Procedure 41 provides procedures applicable to search warrants to obtain evidence of a crime; contraband, fruits of crime, or other items illegally possessed; or property "designed for use, intended for use, or used in committing a crime."[41]

During the indictment phase, federal grand juries have the power to investigate the possibility that a federal crime has been committed within the judicial district in which they are convened and enjoy the benefit of the subpoena power of the court within whose district they sit. [42] However, grand jury subpoenas are limited. Namely, like criminal search warrants, their purpose must have a criminal nexus.

Other subpoena authorities include those issued during the discovery or trial phases of a criminal prosecution and those issued by federal agencies pursuant to specific statutes.[43] Although they are analogous to authorities relied upon to acquire third party documents in national security or foreign intelligence gathering investigations, agency administrative subpoenas and grand jury subpoenas are unlikely to provide an alternative means to acquire third party documents in a national security investigation and thus have not been a significant issue in post 9/11 legislation.[44]

Electronic Communications Privacy Act (ECPA)

The Electronic Communications Privacy Act (ECPA) provides three sets of general prohibitions accompanied by law enforcement exceptions that operate under judicial supervision.[45] These address (1) the interception of wire, oral or electronic communications (wiretapping),[46] (2) access to the content of stored electronic communications and to communications transaction records;[47] and (3) the use of trap and trace devices and pen registers (essentially in and out secret "caller id" devices).[48]

ECPA generally prohibits interception of wire, oral, or electronic communications by means of an electronic, mechanical or other device but sets forth a number of exceptions to the general prohibition.[49] It limits the types of criminal cases in which electronic surveillance may be used and requires court orders authorizing electronic surveillance to be supported by probable cause to believe that the target is engaged in criminal activities, that normal investigative techniques are insufficient, and that the facilities that are the subject of surveillance will be used by the target.[50] It also limits the use and dissemination of information intercepted.[51] In addition, when an interception order expires, authorities must notify those whose communications have been intercepted.[52] Moreover, it declares that the FISA and ECPA procedures are the exclusive means for accomplishing electronic surveillance as defined in FISA and for intercepting wire, oral, or electronic communications.[53]

Whereas provisions governing interception of communications in criminal investigations reflect a concern for Fourth Amendment requirements,[54] portions of ECPA which address stored communications and the use of pen registers and trap and trace devices are less demanding and reflect Supreme Court jurisprudence suggesting that third party business records and communications entrusted to third parties are not typically protected.[55] Government authorities may have access to communications stored with providers, and related communications records, under a search warrant, subpoena, or court order,[56] or when voluntarily surrendered by providers in emergency circumstances.[57] However, as with the interception of communications, ECPA limits the government's use and dissemination of information and requires that targets be notified.[58]

Foreign Intelligence Surveillance Act (FISA)

FISA governs the gathering of information about foreign powers, including international terrorist organizations such as al Qaeda, and their agents.[59] Although it is often discussed in relation to the prevention of terrorism, it applies to the gathering of foreign intelligence information for other purposes.[60]

Although some exceptions apply,[61] government agencies typically must obtain authorization from the Foreign Intelligence Surveillance Court (FISC), a neutral judicial decision maker, when gathering foreign intelligence information pursuant to FISA. Orders issued by the FISC authorize federal officials to conduct electronic surveillance[62] or physical searches;[63] utilize pen registers and trap and trace devices;[64] access specified business records and other tangible things;[65] or target U.S. persons reasonably believed to be abroad.[66]

Although requiring a nexus to a foreign power or foreign intelligence is a common theme, different standards apply for each type of FISA order. For electronic surveillance orders, FISA currently requires that an application include, among other things, a "statement of the facts and circumstances relied upon" to justify the government's belief that a target is a foreign power or its agent.[67] It must also describe the identity, if known, or a description of the specific target of the electronic surveillance and the nature and location of each of the facilities or places at which the electronic surveillance will be directed, if known.[68] When the nature and location are unknown, the FISC must direct the relevant officials to provide notice to the FISC of specific information within 10 days of the date on which surveillance begins to be directed at a new facility or place.[69] FISA also requires that less intrusive means of information gathering be used before an electronic surveillance order may be granted. Specifically, an application for an order authorizing electronic surveillance must include a certification that the information sought under the order is foreign intelligence information, and that the information may not reasonably be obtained by normal investigative techniques, together with a statement of the basis upon which such certifications rest.[70] Relatedly, an application for an electronic surveillance order must specify proposed "minimization procedures."[71]

For physical searches, the government typically must provide, among other things, "the identity, if known, or a description of the target of the search," and "a statement of the facts and circumstances relied upon by the applicant to justify the applicant's belief that ... the target of the physical search is a foreign power or an agent of a foreign power."[72]

For FISA orders authorizing pen registers and trap and trace devices, although limited exceptions apply,[73] an application generally must certify that "the information likely to be obtained is foreign intelligence information not concerning a United States person or is relevant to an ongoing investigation to protect against international terrorism or clandestine intelligence activities."[74]

Finally, for orders to access records and other tangible things, FISA currently requires both "a statement of facts showing that there are reasonable grounds to believe that the tangible things sought are relevant to a [foreign intelligence, international terrorism, or espionage investigation]" and an "enumeration of minimization procedures" to be applied.[75] These provisions also include recipient non-disclosure provisions, grounds for recipients to challenge such production or nondisclosure requirements, and government reporting requirements.[76]

Many of these statutes include a requirement intended to safeguard individuals' freedom of speech and other First Amendment protections. In particular, investigations generally must not be based solely on a U.S. citizen's exercise of his or her First Amendment rights.[77]

National Security Letter Statutes

Five federal statutes require businesses—namely communications providers, financial institutions, and consumer credit entities—to produce specified records to federal officials in national security investigations.[78] Absent a statutory prohibition or some other specific legal impediment, federal authorities are free to request, and to receive voluntarily, access to third party business records. These national security letter (NSL) statutes are designed to carve out narrow national security exceptions to prohibitions on government information gathering in ECPA, the Right to Financial Privacy Act, and the Fair Credit Reporting Act.

Unlike with warrants in criminal investigations or orders issued under FISA, NSLs are issued directly by federal officials, without approval by any judicial body. They are analogous to orders for tangible things issued in intelligence gathering investigations pursuant to FISA because they are a demand for business records and their use is confined to national security investigations. Yet unlike FISA orders, they are not issued by a court and are available for only the records of three narrow categories of businesses. Moreover, the FBI issues tens of thousands of NSLs a year,[79] while the FISA court approves only a handful of tangible-item orders a year.[80]

Only the FBI may issue NSLs under the communications provider, financial institution, and the narrower of the two consumer credit agency statutes. Authority under the other consumer credit agency statute is available to the agencies of the intelligence community, and authority under the National Security Act extends to both intelligence and law enforcement agencies.

The information available under each of the statutes varies. The National Security Act statute reaches an extensive array of financial and consumer credit records, but only applies to federal employees and individuals who have consented to disclosure of the information.[81] The more sweeping consumer credit statute extends to any consumer information held by a consumer credit reporting agency but only when sought in connection with an investigation into international terrorism.[82] The communications provider NSL statute applies to provider transaction records concerning customers' names, addresses, length of service, and billing records sought in connection with an inquiry into international terrorism or clandestine intelligence activities.[83] The more circumspect of the consumer credit NSL statutes covers credit agency records concerning consumers' names, current and former addresses, current and former places of employment, and the identification of financial institutions in which they have or had accounts—sought in connection with an inquiry into international terrorism and clandestine intelligence activities.[84] The financial institution NSL statute reaches customer transaction records of banks, credit unions, and a long list of other businesses that often deal in cash (pawn shops, casinos, car dealerships, jewelers, etc.), again sought in connection with an inquiry into international terrorism and clandestine intelligence activities.[85]

NSL recipients may be bound by nondisclosure requirements under each of the statutes.[86] However, they may seek judicial review of any secrecy requirement imposed and of the NSL itself.[87]

Changes Made by the USA PATRIOT Act and Subsequent Measures

The USA PATRIOT Act and subsequent measures made far-reaching changes expanding the government's authority to collect private information pursuant to FISA, ECPA, and the NSL statutes.[88] Absent congressional intervention, three of the amendments to FISA—the lone wolf, roving wiretap, and business record provisions—will expire on February 28, 2011.

Lowering of the Wall between Criminal Investigations and Foreign Intelligence Gathering

The USA PATRIOT Act lowered somewhat the wall traditionally separating criminal investigation from foreign intelligence gathering. Prior to the act, FISA required that foreign intelligence gathering be the sole or primary purpose of an investigation; thus, activities conducted with an additional rationale of criminal investigation were required to adhere to criminal procedure requirements. Section 218 of the act amended the standard to require that foreign intelligence gathering be a "significant" rather than "the

[sole]" purpose of surveillance or a search for which a court order is sought under FISA.[89] Thus, the presence of ancillary criminal investigation purposes no longer eliminates the ability to rely on FISA authorities, so long as a significant foreign intelligence purpose also exists. Relatedly, as discussed *infra*, the USA PATRIOT Act and subsequent measures increased the scope of international terrorism-related activities which now fall within the ambit of the federal criminal code.

The act also attempted to improve communication between foreign intelligence and criminal law enforcement agencies. To that end, it includes several provisions that authorize information sharing. For example, section 504 authorizes federal officers to consult with criminal law enforcement officers regarding information obtained from a physical search in order "to coordinate efforts to investigate or protect against" various national security threats.[90]

Expansion of Persons Subject to Investigation

Several post-9/11 measures addressed threshold or definitional issues affecting the range of persons whose communications, records, or effects might be investigated as part of foreign intelligence gathering. The controversial 2004 lone wolf provision, one of the three expiring provisions, is especially significant. It expanded the definition of "agent of a foreign power" in FISA to include a non-U.S. person who "knowingly engages in sabotage or international terrorism, or activities that are in preparation therefor, for or on behalf of a foreign power."[91] Because FISA orders—including those for surveillance, physical searches, pen registers, trap and trace devices, and business records—require evidence indicating that a target is a foreign power or its agent, the broadened definition makes the authorities applicable to targets for which a link to an international terrorist organization or other foreign power is not yet supported by probable cause.[92]

Another important expansion followed in the wake of revelations regarding the Terrorist Surveillance Program. Two measures, discussed in greater detail *infra*,[93] eased federal officials' ability to gather foreign intelligence information between persons in the United States and others thought to be located outside of the United States. In the first, now expired, measure, Congress exempted "surveillance directed at a person reasonably believed to be located outside of the United States" from the definition of "electronic surveillance" under FISA.[94] Although this made it unnecessary to obtain a FISA order to conduct such surveillance, Congress simultaneously established temporary procedures governing the capture of communications for specified groups of targets reasonably believed to be located overseas.[95] The second measure provides separate authorities with differing standards for targeting non-U.S. persons and U.S. persons reasonably believed to be located outside the United States. [96]

Finally, by authorizing the collection of information believed to be *relevant to* a national security or foreign intelligence investigation, the USA PATRIOT Act and its successors in several instances widened the circle of persons whose communications or effects might fall within the ambit of authorities for intelligence gathering.[97] Authorities had previously limited that circle to persons believed to be agents of foreign powers.

Expansion of Electronic Surveillance Authorities

The USA PATRIOT Act amended electronic surveillance authorities in ECPA and FISA. The amendments to ECPA primarily address matters other than the interception of the content of communications. However, the act did add several terrorism-related offenses to the list of federal crimes that may serve as the basis for an interception order.[98] It also authorizes intercepting officers to share information with various federal intelligence and law enforcement officials[99] and provides explicit disciplinary provisions for intentional violations by federal employees.[100]

Moreover, section 217 created a new exception to ECPA's general prohibition on the interception of electronic communications. The exception permits law enforcement officials to intercept the communications of an intruder into someone else's computer or computer system with the consent of system's owner or operator.[101] The exception is limited to the trespasser's communications to, through, and from the invaded system.

An additional important amendment to ECPA broadened the stored communication language in an effort to treat stored voice mail in the same manner as e-mail.[102] Finally, section 220 amended ECPA to permit nationwide service of search warrants of material held by service providers,[103] and section 212 amended it to allow for emergency disclosures by service providers.[104]

Likewise, the USA PATRIOT Act and its progeny made several changes to FISA's electronic surveillance authorities. The so-called "roving wiretap" provision, section 206 of the USA PATRIOT Act, permits roving or multipoint wiretaps where the Foreign Intelligence Surveillance Court finds

that the actions of the target of the application for electronic surveillance under FISA may have the effect of thwarting the identification of a specific communications or other common carrier, landlord, custodian, or specified person to whom the order to furnish information, facilities, or technical assistance in connection with the wiretap should be directed.[105] As amended by P.L. 109-177, this finding must be based upon specific facts provided in the application.[106] In addition, section 207 of the USA PATRIOT Act extended the duration of FISA wiretaps and extensions thereof.[107]

Section 225 added a new provision to FISA that bars suits against any wire or electronic service provider, custodian, landlord, or other person that furnishes information, facilities, or technical assistance in connection with electronic surveillance pursuant to a FISC order or with a request for emergency assistance under FISA.[108]

Expansion of Authorities to Conduct Physical Searches

"Physical searches," as defined by FISA, are analogous to searches authorized by warrants in criminal investigations.[109] The most notable amendment specific to FISA provisions governing orders for physical searches, made by section 207 of the USA PATRIOT Act, increased the maximum duration of physical search orders targeting persons other than a foreign power.[110] The maximum duration of such orders was 45 days but is now 120 days for searches targeting an agent of a foreign power and 90 days for other targets.[111]

Expansion of Authorities for Pen Registers and Trap and Trace Devices

The USA PATRIOT Act amended both FISA and ECPA provisions relevant to the use of pen register and trap and trace devices. The most notable amendment to FISA was made in section 214. Previously, the use of pen registers and similar devices could be authorized only for investigations to gather foreign intelligence information or information concerning international terrorism. Section 214 broadened the purposes for which the devices may be authorized by allowing their use in "any investigation to obtain foreign intelligence information not concerning a United States person or to protect against international terrorism or clandestine intelligence activities."[112] However, it prohibits any investigation involving a United States person that is "conducted solely upon the basis of activities protected by the first amendment to the Constitution."[113]

Section 216 amended the ECPA to authorize courts to issue orders for the use of pen registers and trap and trace devices anywhere within the United States.[114] The statute previously limited their application to the issuing court's jurisdiction. It also authorizes the use of such devices to capture source and addressee information for computer conversations (e.g., e-mail) as well as telephone conversations.[115]

Expanded Access to Records and Other Tangible Things

As mentioned, the USA PATRIOT Act focused in part on the statutory tools available in anti-terrorism investigations. Some of those tools enable agents to unearth documents that reveal the paper trail of crime and of the activities of international terrorist organizations and other foreign powers and their agents—grand jury, administrative, and judicial subpoenas; search warrants; court orders under the Electronic Communications Privacy Act (ECPA) and the Foreign Intelligence Surveillance Act (FISA); and national security letters (NSLs). The most important changes were made to FISA and the national security letter statutes. The USA PATRIOT Act and the related legislation that followed sought to make those implements more effective within a system of reinforced civil liberties safeguards.

National Security Letters

The USA PATRIOT Act expanded authorities for agency-issued national security letters. It authorized their issuance with the approval of the Special Agents in Charge of FBI field offices (SACs); broadened the range of permissible targets; and enacted the community-wide-all-consumer credit-information national security letter statute.[116] Prior to the USA PATRIOT Act, the national security letter statutes permitted issuance only upon government certification of specific and articulable facts, giving reason to believe that the information sought pertained to a foreign power or one of its agents.[117] Now, they require a certification that the information is relevant to, or is sought for, a particular national security investigation.[118] The change means that national security letters may be issued at a stage in the investigation when the precise relationship (if any) of a subject to a specific terrorist organization or other

foreign power has yet to be established. It also means that information is more likely to be gathered from people several steps removed from a foreign power or its agents and is more likely to pertain to individuals not ultimately of interest.

Reports of the inspector general of the Department of Justice indicate that the FBI previously did not find pre-amendment national security letters particularly useful but now considers them indispensable.[119] Information gleaned from national security letter responses is used to produce analytical intelligence reports; further investigations; provide the basis for FISA orders and pursue other investigative techniques; and help decide whether to open, continue, or close an investigation or line of inquiry.[120] However, the inspector general also found that, at least initially, "the FBI used national security letters in violation of applicable national security letter statutes, Attorney General Guidelines, and internal FBI policies."[121]

FISA Orders for Business Records and Other Tangible Things

Section 215 of the USA PATRIOT Act, one of the three amendments to FISA scheduled to expire on February 28, 2011, was perhaps the act's most controversial provision. It expanded the authority for FISA orders compelling records and other tangible things in two ways. First, it enlarged the scope of materials that may be sought. Prior to the enactment of the USA PATRIOT Act, FISA authorized court orders for access to only four types of business records: car rental records, housing accommodation (e.g., hotel/motel) records, storage rental records, and travel (e.g., airline/train) records.[122] As amended, the section authorizes the FISC to issue orders for access to "any tangible things." [123] Second, the section lowered the standard which must be met before the court may issue such orders. The previous standard required a showing of specific and articulable facts giving reason to believe the information related to a foreign power or the agent of a foreign power. As amended, the provision now requires "a statement of facts showing that there are reasonable grounds to believe that the tangible things sought are relevant to a [foreign intelligence, international terrorism, or espionage investigation.]"[124]

Specific concerns regarding the provision's potential application to library records and other materials thought to be particularly private or sensitive prompted further revisions to the relevant FISA authorities. In 2006, Congress modified the tangible item provisions to restrict the officials who may apply for orders covering library, bookstore, gun sale, tax or medical records to senior FBI headquarters officials; for other types of materials, FBI field office SACs may also apply.[125]

The 2006 measures also called for audits of the use of section 215 authority by the Justice Department's inspector general.[126] The resulting reports indicate that the authority was exercised only relatively infrequently and most often in part to secure information that is now available under FISA trap and trace authority.[127] Prior to the 2006 amendments, FISA trap and trace authority did not permit the order to include a demand for related customer record information, a problem authorities overcame by submitting a FISA tangible item order request in combination with a FISA trap and trace order request.[128] The 2006 amendments enlarged FISA trap and trace authority so that such "combo" FISA applications are no longer necessary.[129] The FISA court approved six "pure" section 215 requests in 2004; 14 in 2005; 15 in 2006; 17 in 2007; and 18 in 2008.[130] The IG reports suggest several reasons for the sparse use. The approval process is less familiar, multi-layered, sometimes cumbersome, and time consuming.[131] Moreover, voluntary compliance, NSLs, grand jury subpoenas, or FISA trap and trace orders can often provide access to the same documents more quickly.[132] Nevertheless, the Justice Department considers section 215 authority to be a valuable tool when these alternative means are not available.[133]

A final important change affected the burden of proof for the standard of relevancy. Record checks are often the "stuff" of running down leads. Before 2006, FISA tangible-item orders were available when "sought" for certain national security investigations—that is, sometimes to determine whether they would be relevant, not because they were determined to be relevant.[134] In such cases, FISA responses not infrequently included irrelevant information. After the 2006 amendments, the orders authorize government access only to relevant information.[135] However, records are declared "presumptively relevant" if they pertain to a foreign power or one of its agents, to the suspected agent who is the subject of the investigation, or to an individual in contact with, or known to, such an agent.[136] The relevancy presumption seems to make acquisition of information pertaining to "innocent" Americans more likely. Foreign agents may "know" many people, some involved in their nefarious activities, others not. The amendment creates a presumption of relevancy for information pertaining to both groups.

New Statutory Authority to Conduct "Sneak and Peek" Searches

As a general rule, the Federal Rules of Criminal Procedure require officers executing a search warrant to give notice that they have done so and to leave an inventory of the property they have seized.[137] Section 213 of the USA PATRIOT Act, as amended, permits delayed notice search warrants under some circumstances.[138] A delayed notice, or "sneak and peek," search warrant is one that authorizes law enforcement officers to secretly enter a home or business, either physically or virtually, conduct a search, take pictures or copy documents, and depart without taking any tangible evidence or leaving notice of their presence. Before section 213, the federal courts agreed that such warrants might be issued under certain exigent circumstances, but disagreed over whether an unnoticed search in the absence of sufficient exigent circumstances constituted a Fourth Amendment violation as well as a violation of the federal rules. They also disagreed as to whether notice might be delayed for longer than seven days or some similar short period of time without court approval.[139]

The law now permits a delayed notification for 30 days or more for such warrants. In addition, the period of delay may be renewed and extended for intervals of 90 days or more if there is reason to believe that immediate notification will "result in (A) endangering the life or physical safety of an individual; (B) flight from prosecution; (C) destruction of or tampering with evidence; (D) intimidation of potential witnesses; or (E) otherwise seriously jeopardizing an investigation."[140]

In FY2008, federal courts issued 763 delayed notice warrants, most often for 90 days.[141] Drug cases accounted for 474 of the initial warrants and for 369 of the 528 extensions granted; terrorism cases accounted for three of the warrants and two of the extensions.[142] Thus, even when there is a criminal nexus, delayed notice search warrants do not appear to be a regular employed investigative tool in national security investigations.

Judicial Oversight and Minimization Procedures

Congress relies on three types of safeguards to protect against abuse of the new authority established by the USA PATRIOT Act and its successors: congressional oversight, judicial oversight, and minimization procedures.

Congressional Oversight

Measures following the USA PATRIOT Act established various reporting and notification requirements, presumably to provide transparency regarding the use of enhanced authorities. For example, section 6002 of the FISA Amendments Act of 2004, P.L. 108-458, requires the Attorney General, on a semiannual basis, to report to relevant committees regarding the use of various FISA authorities, Foreign Intelligence Surveillance Court decisions, and related matters for each preceding six-month period.[143]

Congress instituted additional reporting requirements when it reauthorized and made permanent many USA PATRIOT Act provisions in 2005. For example, section 114 of the USA PATRIOT Improvement and Reauthorization Act of 2005 enhanced congressional oversight of delayed notice search warrants by requiring that no later than 30 days after the expiration or denial of such a warrant, the issuing or denying judge notify the Administrative Office of the U.S. Courts of (1) an application for a delayed notice search warrant; (2) whether the warrant was either granted, modified, or denied; (3) the length of time of the delay in giving notice; and (4) the offense specified in the warrant or the application.[144] In addition, it requires the Director of the Administrative Office to submit an annual report to Congress summarizing the use of delayed notice warrants.[145]

Similarly, section 209 of the 2005 reauthorization measure instituted a semi-annual reporting requirement, whereby the Attorney General must report to the Senate Judiciary Committee and the House and Senate Intelligence Committees regarding physical searches conducted pursuant to FISA, and must submit to those committees and the House Judiciary Committee a report with statistical information concerning the number of emergency physical search orders authorized or denied by the Attorney General.[146] Likewise, section 128 requires that the Judiciary Committees receive full reports on the use of the FISA's pen register and trap and trace authority every six months.[147]

Judicial Oversight

Notification requirements facilitate judicial oversight as well. For example, section 216 of the USA PATRIOT Act requires law enforcement officers to submit a detailed report to the court authorizing the search describing information collected via pen registers and trap and trace devices.[148] The requirement was likely a response to objections that e-mail header information, now authorized to be collected, can be more revealing than a telephone number.

Congress and the courts have also addressed individuals' direct access to judicial review. For example, section 223 of the USA PATRIOT Act amended ECPA to authorize a cause of action against the United States for willful violation by federal employees of the stored communications and records provisions, of the court-ordered interception provisions, and of the FISA electronic surveillance, physical search, pen register, or trap and trace device provisions.[149]

The federal courts have in some cases determined that insufficient access to judicial review raises constitutional problems. In the context of national security letters, the U.S. Court of Appeals for the Second Circuit, in *John Doe, Inc. v. Mukasey,*[150] held that the current gag order and accompanying judicial review provisions only survive First Amendment scrutiny if the government takes specified actions. Namely, it must promptly petition for judicial review (at the recipient's option) and convince the district court that the proposed secrecy provision is narrowly crafted to meet the statutorily identified adverse consequences of disclosure.[151] The *John Doe, Inc.* court also found unconstitutional the statutory requirement (18 U.S.C. § 3511(b)) that a reviewing court give conclusive weight to the government's certification that disclosure might have adverse consequences.[152]

Judicial review of nondisclosure orders accompanying FISA tangible items orders would seem to stand on different footing. The First Amendment defect in the NSL provisions is the want of prompt judicial involvement. The nondisclosure orders under FISA are issued by the FISC, a neutral judicial body, and consequently would seem to suffer no such malady. The statute, however, establishes an intricate procedure under which a recipient must wait a year before filing a motion to modify or set aside a nondisclosure requirement.[153] Petitions, which survive a screening process designed to weed out frivolous challenges, may be granted only if the judge concludes that there is no reason to believe that disclosure would endanger national security or individual safety or would interfere with a diplomatic relations or a criminal, counter-terrorism, or counter-intelligence investigation.[154] As in the NSL statute provision to which the Second Circuit objected,[155] the government's certification of a possible adverse impact on national security or diplomatic relations is conclusive.[156] If a petition is denied, a renewed petition may not be filed until a year later.[157]

Although FISA does not say so in so many words, the recipient of a FISA order who disobeys an order of the court probably stands in contempt of court.[158] It may be assumed that FISA court-issued orders would be beyond reproach on First Amendment grounds when issued. Yet, the time bars on release from a gag order for which the need has passed might be thought troubling. The time bars notwithstanding, however, a recipient might find an effective avenue for timely review by refusing to comply with the order to produce followed by a challenge to the gag order at the subsequent show cause or habeas hearing.

Minimization Procedures

Minimization means different things in different contexts. In an abstract sense, it means capturing, keeping, using, and passing on to others no more information than is necessary to satisfy the purposes for which the statutory authority to do so was given. Under ECPA, it means procedures to minimize the interception of communications other than those for which the Title III order was granted.[159] Under FISA, minimization means, roughly, procedures to curtail the interception of the communications of Americans consistent with national security needs.[160] FISA also has provisions governing the use of FISA-generated evidence in subsequent federal or state proceedings under which district courts may review the legality of the use of FISA authority and suppress the resulting evidence when appropriate.[161] As discussed *supra*, in addition to requiring minimization procedures specific to an investigation, both ECPA and FISA also place general limitations on the use of authorities and the information collected. For example, ECPA restricts the use and dissemination of information collected.[162]

Today, the national security letter statutes have no comparable provisions, although most have dissemination limits.[163] Section 119 of the USA PATRIOT Improvement and Reauthorization Act of 2005 directed the Attorney General to report on the feasibility of establishing national security letter minimization procedures.[164] A report prepared by the Justice Department's inspector general discussed efforts of the Justice Department to formulate such procedures and reservations concerning the initial proposals.[165] The inspector general has also testified that such procedures are needed and overdue, but acknowledged that the task has proven challenging.[166] He expressed the view that the national security letter minimization procedures should address "collection of information through national security letters, how the FBI can upload national security information in FBI databases, the dissemination of NSL information, the appropriate tagging and tracking of national security letter derived information in FBI databases and files, and the time period for retention of national security letter obtained information."[167]

Unlike the NSL statutes, section 215 of the USA PATRIOT Act, as amended, has an explicit minimization component, which calls for procedures governing the retention and dissemination of records and other tangible things collected pursuant to FISA orders.[168] The Justice Department, however, failed to reach internal consensus on issues such as "the time period for retention of information, definitional issues of 'U.S. person identifying information,' and whether to include procedures for addressing material received in response to, but beyond the scope of, the FISA Court order; uploading information into FBI databases; and handling large or sensitive data collections."[169] Accordingly, it issued interim procedures, which the inspector general concluded "do not adequately address the intent and requirements of the [law] for minimization requirements."[170]

RELATED MATTERS

A few key ancillary matters are likely to be raised in the legislative debate surrounding reauthorization of the USA PATRIOT Act and related authorities. One is the increasingly murky relationship between intelligence gathering authorities and the federal criminal code. Provisions enacted in the wake of the Terrorist Surveillance Program, including retroactive immunity for communications providers and authorities regarding persons located outside the United States that are set to expire in 2012 may also be explored.

Nexus between Intelligence Gathering and Federal Criminal Statutes

Despite some lessening of traditional divisions between criminal law enforcement and foreign intelligence gathering resulting from the USA PATRIOT Act and subsequent measures, the purpose of government activity, and the resulting statutory framework, continues to have important consequences for the scope and nature of information collection likely to be authorized. Searches and surveillance in criminal investigations must be justified by indicia of criminal conduct.[171] In contrast, a significant purpose of an electronic surveillance or a physical search conducted pursuant to FISA must be the collection of foreign intelligence information,[172] and those activities must be supported by probable cause to believe both (1) that the person targeted by the order is a foreign power or its agent, and (2) that the subject of the search (i.e., the telecommunications at which the surveillance is directed or place to be searched) is owned, possessed, in transit to or from, or is being or is about to be used by the target.[173] Likewise, the use of national security letters is generally limited to investigations of international terrorism or for clandestine intelligence activities.

Thus, the presence of a criminal law enforcement rationale is significant. Federal intelligence agents may avail themselves of grand jury subpoenas and other criminal law enforcement tools when there is a nexus to a criminal offense. The existence of that nexus often depends upon the reach of federal substantive anti-terrorism law. Federal law prohibits certain violent acts of terrorism such as aircraft sabotage and the use of weapons of mass destruction.[174] It also condemns misconduct committed in anticipation of violent acts of terrorism such as providing material support to terrorism organizations or accepting military training from terrorist organizations.[175] Moreover, terrorist offenses often serve as an element of other federal crimes such as racketeering or supply the basis for expanded procedural options in areas such as the statute of limitations.[176] For example, federal law extends the general five-year statute of limitations for prosecution of a federal crime to eight years when the offense is one defined as a federal crime of terrorism.[177]

Two federal statutes, both amended by the USA PATRIOT Act, outlaw providing material support for terrorists. One prohibits providing support for federal crimes of terrorism or similar offenses;[178] the other providing support for designated terrorist organizations.[179] The second declares in part that "[w]hoever knowingly provides material support or resources to a foreign terrorist organization, or attempts or conspires to do so, shall be fined under this title or imprisoned not more than 15 years, or both."[180] Conviction requires proof that the defendant either knew that the organization had been designated a foreign terrorist organization or that it engaged in terrorism.[181] It does not require the government to prove that the support was provided with the intent to further the organization's illicit activities.[182] The Ninth Circuit has held that the terms "training" and "service" as used in these sections to describe prohibited forms of material support are unconstitutionally vague.[183] The Supreme Court has agreed to hear arguments which assert that they are incompatible with the prohibitions of the First Amendment and unconstitutionally vague.[184]

In addition to the racketeering and statute of limitation provisions, federal crimes of terrorism appear in a number of federal statutes. In some instances, the presence of a federal crime of terrorism is an element of the offense.[185] In others, investigation of a federal crime of terrorism constitutes an exception to an otherwise applicable privacy restriction.[186] As a general rule, the Sentencing Guidelines recommend more severe sentences for federal crimes of terrorism.[187]

In addition to the material support crime, federal law uses an alternative terrorism cross reference with at least equal regularity. Namely, 18 U.S.C. § 2331 provides an element for some offenses, such as one which makes it a federal crime to commit bribery affecting port security with the intent to commit international or domestic terrorism.[188] It too supplies the grounds for an exception to otherwise binding privacy restrictions.[189] And, several federal crimes are more severely punished when they are committed in furtherance of international or domestic terrorism.[190]

The difference between the two cross references is one of specificity on one hand and a terrorism nexus on the other. 18 U.S.C. § 2332b(g)(5)(B) provides a relatively limited list of specific federal crimes that need not necessarily be committed in a terrorist context.[191] 18 U.S.C. § 2331, on the other hand, includes any federal, state, or foreign crime of violence, but only if committed for terrorist purposes.[192] The domestic terrorism definition of section 2331 originated in the USA PATRIOT Act.[193] Critics have suggested that its want of specificity threatens possible misuse against political dissents.[194]

Aftermath of the Terrorist Surveillance Program (TSP)

In late 2005, the *New York Times* reported that the federal government had "monitored the international telephone calls and international e-mail messages of hundreds, perhaps thousands, of people in the United States without warrants."[195] Subsequently, President Bush acknowledged that, after the attacks of September 11, 2001, he had authorized the National Security Agency to "intercept international communications into and out of the United States" by "persons linked to al Qaeda or related terrorist organizations" based upon "his constitutional authority to conduct warrantless wartime electronic surveillance of the enemy,"[196] despite the general rule that electronic surveillance by the federal government is unlawful unless conducted pursuant to the Foreign Intelligence Surveillance Act (FISA) or Title III of the Omnibus

Crime Control and Safe Streets Act (Title III).[197] Now discontinued, the TSP appears to have been active from shortly after September 11, 2001, to some time in January of 2007.[198]

Following these revelations, Congress enacted the Protect America Act, P.L. 110-55, and the FISA Amendments Act of 2008, P.L. 110-261. They addressed several issues raised in public discussions regarding the TSP. Two provisions likely to arise in the current legislative debate include (1) retroactive immunity for telecommunications providers who played a role in the TSP; and (2) temporary provisions applying different procedures and standards to targets under FISA depending upon the person's nationality and geographic location.

Retroactive Immunity for Telecommunications Providers

After private citizens and interest groups became aware of the TSP, they filed dozens of lawsuits alleging various statutory and constitutional violations by the telecommunications companies that participated in the program.[199] During litigation, the government moved for the dismissal of the cases on the basis of the state secrets privilege, which bars the disclosure during litigation of information that, "in the interest of national security, should not be divulged."[200] While the district court left open the possibility that the privilege might lead to dismissal at a later date, it declined to dismiss the suits before the discovery stage in the litigation.[201]

Insofar as many of the details of the TSP remain classified, it is likely that assertions of the state secrets privilege would have been central to the disposition of the civil suits against telecommunications providers. However, the enactment of the 2008 FISA Amendments Act provided the Attorney General with the authority to seek the dismissal of these lawsuits.[202] Under the 2008 law, no civil case against a covered telecommunications company could proceed if the Attorney General certified that any assistance given by the defendant was given in connection with the TSP between September 11, 2001, and January 17, 2007, and the defendant received written assurances that the TSP was authorized by the President and determined to be lawful.[203] Dismissal was required if the court found that the certified facts were supported by "substantial evidence." In September of 2008, Attorney General Mukasey made the necessary certification and moved to dismiss the civil suits against the telecommunications providers.[204] In June of 2009, the consolidated suits were dismissed after the district court found the certification to be supported by substantial evidence.[205] That decision was appealed to the Ninth Circuit, and is currently pending.

Were Congress to act subsequently to repeal the retroactive immunity provided by the FAA, the defendants might argue that such a repeal violates their due process rights[206] or the constitutionally required separation of powers.[207] However, courts have generally only upheld such claims where the party was in possession of a final, unreviewable judgment. Although, at this time, the cases have been dismissed by the district court, that dismissal has not been reduced to a final, unreviewable judgment as it is currently being reviewed by the Ninth Circuit. Therefore, legislative modification of the retroactive immunity enjoyed by these defendants under the FISA Amendments Act remains a possibility.

Provisions Expiring in 2012

After the TSP activities were concluded in 2007, Congress enacted the Protect America Act, which established a mechanism for the acquisition, via a certification by the Director of National Intelligence (DNI) and the Attorney General but without a court order, of foreign intelligence information concerning a person reasonably believed to be outside the United States.[208] This temporary authority ultimately expired after approximately six months, on February 16, 2008. Several months later, the Congress enacted the FISA Amendments Act of 2008, which created separate procedures for targeting non-U.S. persons and U.S. persons reasonably believed to be outside the United States under a new Title VII of FISA.[209] Title VII is set to expire on December 31, 2012.

Pursuant to Title VII, non-U.S. persons reasonably believed to be abroad may be targeted to acquire foreign intelligence information pursuant to a joint Attorney General/Director of National Intelligence (DNI) authorization if certain criteria are met.[210] The authority may not be used for reverse targeting—in situations where the true focus of the collection effort is a person in the United States.[211] Title VII requires a FISC order to authorize the targeting U.S. persons reasonably believed to be abroad.[212] The targeting procedures, minimization procedures, and supporting certifications by the Attorney General and the DNI, applicable to the targeting of non-U.S. persons reasonably believed to be outside the United States, are subject to judicial review by the FISC. In addition, electronic communications service providers directed by the Attorney General and the DNI to provide assistance in connection with such acquisitions from targeted non-U.S. persons may challenge such directives before the FISC, with appeal to the Foreign Intelligence Surveillance Court of Review, and, if necessary, to the Supreme Court. Probable cause determinations, minimization procedures, and certifications with respect to the targeting of U.S. persons reasonably believed to be outside the United States are also subject to judicial review.

CONCLUSION

As with previous USA PATRIOT Act reauthorization debates, the slated expiration of FISA amendments in 2011 (and provisions concerning persons reasonably believed to be abroad in 2012) may prompt an examination of authorities for government collection of private information. As mentioned, bills introduced in the 111th Congress (before a key expiration date was temporarily extended) propose significant changes to existing authorities. Congress is likely to revisit those proposals when it considers a longer-term extension of expiring provisions.

Arguments raised in the debate in the 111th Congress reflect fundamental questions regarding the level of government intrusion necessary to ensure the country's safety. Referring to the expiring provisions, the U.S. Department of Justice asserts that the expanded authorities have proven to be important and effective intelligence gathering tools.[213] Thus, although it is "willing to consider" proposals to modify authorities to provide additional privacy protections, the Justice Department warns that care should be taken to ensure that any changes to existing authorities "do not undermine the effectiveness of [the expiring FISA amendments]."[214]

Countervailing arguments assert that amendments enacted following the 9/11 terrorist attacks undermined citizens' civil liberties unnecessarily.[215] Specifically, they argue that the broader the authorities for the collection of foreign intelligence information, the greater the likelihood that U.S. citizens' private conversations or documents will be swept within the scope of an authorized investigation. For example, a concern might be that the authority for "roving wiretaps" increases the likelihood that innocent conversations involving U.S. citizens will be the subject of electronic surveillance. Likewise, at least one commentator asserts that national security letters have a "too diffuse" focus, which leads to anecdotal evidence showing that "their effectiveness is disproportionately small compared with the extent of ... the invasion of privacy they represent."[216]

Reflecting the arguments on both sides, the legislative debate is likely to address ways in which the need for rigorous investigative tools might be balanced with the safeguarding of constitutional guarantees.

End Notes

[1] Uniting and Strengthening America by Providing Appropriate Tools Required to Intercept and Obstruct Terrorism (USA PATRIOT) Act of 2001, P.L. 107-56; H.Rept. 107-236, pt. 1, at 41 (2001).

[2] *See, e.g., Reauthorizing the USA PATRIOT Act: Ensuring Liberty and Security: Hearing Before the S. Judiciary Comm.*, 111th Cong. (Sept. 23, 2009) (statement of Kenneth L. Wainstein, Partner, O'Melveny & Myers and former Ass't Atty'y Gen. for National Security).

[3] *See, e.g., Unchecked National Security Letter Powers and Our Civil Liberties: Hearing Before the House Perm. Select Comm. on Intelligence*, 110th Cong. (Mar. 28, 2007) (statement of Lisa Graves, then Deputy Director, Center for National Security Studies).

[4] *See, e.g.*, USA PATRIOT Improvement and Reauthorization Act of 2005, P.L. 109-177; An act to amend the USA PATRIOT Act to extend the sunset of certain provisions of that act to July 1, 2006, P.L. 109-160; USA PATRIOT Act Additional Reauthorizing Amendments Act of 2006, P.L. 109-178; Protect America Act of 2007, P.L. 110-55; FISA Amendments Act of 2008, P.L. 110-261.

[5] Additional relevant proposals include, for example, S. 1686, S. 1725, S. 1726, S. 2336, H.R. 1800, H.R. 3846, H.R. 3969, and H.R. 4005.

[6] Although the three expiring provisions are thought of as the "expiring Patriot Act provisions," *see, e.g., Reauthorizing the USA PATRIOT Act: Ensuring Liberty and Security: Hearing Before the Senate Comm. on the Judiciary*, 111th Cong. (Sept. 23, 2009) (statement of Sen. Leahy), only two of the three expiring provisions were enacted in the Patriot Act. *See* P.L. 107-56, § 206, 50 U.S.C. § 1805(c)(2)(B) (known as the "roving wiretap" provision); *Id.* at § 215, 50 U.S.C. §§ 1861-2 (known as the "business records" or "library" provision). The third provision, known as the "lone wolf" provision, is Section 6001(a) of the Intelligence Reform and Terrorism Protection Act (IRTPA). P.L. 108-458, 50 U.S.C. § 1801(b)(1)(C).

[7] P.L. 111-141 (extending the date for the expiring provisions from February 28, 2010, to February 28, 2011). *See also* Department of Defense Appropriations Act, 2010, P.L. 111-118, § 1004 (extending the date for the expiring provisions from December 31, 2009, to February 28, 2010).

[8] U.S. Const. amend. IV.

[9] Kyllo v. United States, 533 U.S. 27, 33 (2001) (citing California v. Ciraolo, 476 U.S. 207, 211 (1986)).

[10] *See, e.g.*, Atwater v. City of Lago Vista, 532 U.S. 318, 354 (2001) (recognizing a warrant exception for arrest of an individual who commits a crime in an officer's presence, as long as the arrest is supported by probable cause). Probable cause is "a fluid concept—turning on the assessment of probabilities in particular factual contexts." Illinois v. Gates, 462 U.S. 213, 232 (1983). For example, for issuance of a search warrant, probable cause requires an issuing magistrate to determine, based on specific evidence, whether there exists a "fair probability" that, for example, an area contains contraband. *Id.* at 238. Exceptions to the warrant requirement include, for example, "exigent circumstances" where people's lives are at risk or illegal items in "plain view" during a search authorized for other items.

[11] Katz v. United States, 389 U.S. 347, 353 (1967), *overruling* Olmstead v. United States, 277 U.S. 438 (1928).

[12] United States v. U.S. District Court, 407 U.S. 297, 313-14, 321-24 (1972) (also referred to as the *Keith* case, so named for the District Court judge who initially ordered disclosure of unlawful warrantless electronic surveillance to the defendants). *See also* In re Directives, 551 F.3d 1004, 1011 (Foreign Intell. Surveillance Ct. Rev. 2008) (holding that the foreign intelligence surveillance of targets reasonably believed to be outside of the U.S. qualifies for the "special needs" exception to the warrant requirement).

[13] In re Sealed Case, 310 F.3d 717, 738-46 (Foreign Intell. Surveillance Ct. Rev. 2002).

[14] The "general reasonableness," or "totality-of-the circumstances," test requires a court to determine the constitutionality of a search or seizure "by assessing, on the one hand, the degree to which [a search or seizure] intrudes upon an individual's privacy and, on the other, the degree to which it is needed for the promotion of legitimate governmental interests." Samson v. California, 547 U.S. 843, 848 (2006).

[15] United States v. Miller, 425 U.S. 435 (1976).

[16] Smith v. Maryland, 442 U.S. 735, 745-46 (1979).

[17] U.S. Const. amend. I.

[18] *See U.S. District Court*, 407 U.S. at 314 ("The price of lawful public dissent must not be a dread of subjection to an unchecked surveillance power. Nor must the fear of unauthorized official eavesdropping deter vigorous citizen dissent and discussion of Government action in private conversation. For private dissent, no less than open public discourse, is essential to our free society.").

[19] *See, e.g.*, 50 U.S.C. § 1842(c).

[20] *See, e.g.*, Office of the Inspector General, Department of Justice, *A Review of the FBI's Use of Section 215 Orders for Business Records in 2006*, Mar. 2008, http://www.usdoj.gov/oig/special/s0803a/final.pdf, at 5 (expressing concern that the FBI had issued a national security letter after the FISA court had twice declined to grant an order for the same material due to First Amendment objections).

[21] P.L. 90-351, 18 U.S.C. §§ 2510-2520 (1970 ed. Supp.IV).

[22] P.L. 99-508, 18 U.S.C. §§ 2510-2520 (1988 ed. Supp.II).

[23] *See* S. Rept. 95-604(I), at 7, 1978 U.S.C.C.A.N. 3904, 3908.

[24] The report of a congressional committee convened to examine intelligence gathering after Watergate stated: "Too many people have been spied upon by too many government agencies and too much information has been collected. The government has often undertaken the secret surveillance of citizens on the basis of their political beliefs, even when those beliefs posed no threat of violence or illegal acts on behalf of a hostile foreign power. The Government, operating primarily through secret informants, but also using other intrusive techniques such as wiretaps, microphone 'bugs', surreptitious mail opening, and break-ins, has swept in vast amounts of information about the personal lives, views, and associations of American citizens." *See Intelligence Activities and the Rights of Americans, Final Report of the Select Committee to Study Governmental Operations with respect to Intelligence Activities and the Rights of Americans, United States Senate, Book II,* S. Rept. 94-755, at 5 (1976) (hereinafter Church Committee Final Report). *See also Supplementary Detailed Staff Reports on Intelligence Activities and the Rights of Americans, Church Committee Final Report,, Book III*, S. Rept. 94-755, at 271-351.

[25] P.L. 95-511, 50 U.S.C. § 1801 *et seq.*

[26] P.L. 95-630, § 1114, 12 U.S.C. § 3401 *et seq.*

[27] 12 U.S.C. § 3414(a)(1)(A), (B).

[28] P.L. 99-569, § 404, 12 U.S.C. § 3414(a)(5)(A).

[29] Electronic Communications Privacy Act, P.L. 99-508, § 201(a), 18 U.S.C. § 2709.

[30] P.L. 103-359, § 802, 50 U.S.C. § 436.

[31] P.L. 104-93, § 601(a), 15 U.S.C. § 1681u.

[32] P.L. 103-359, § 807(a)(3), 50 U.S.C. §§ 1821-1829.

[33] Pen registers capture the numbers dialed on a telephone line; trap and trace devices identify the originating number of an incoming call on a particular phone line. *See* 18 U.S.C. § 3127(3)-(4).

[34] P.L. 105-272, §§ 601, 602.

[35] P.L. 107-56.

[36] *Id.* at § 224.

[37] P.L. 108-458, § 6001.

[38] P.L. 109-177, § 102(a).

[39] *Id.* at §§ 102(b), 103.

[40] Department of Defense Appropriations Act, 2010, P.L. 111-118, § 1004 (extending the expiration date to February 28, 2010); P.L. 111-141 (extending the date to February 28, 2011).

[41] Fed. R. Crim. Pro. 41(c). *See also* 18 U.S.C. § 3103a (adding to the grounds provided in Rule 41 that "a warrant may be issued to search for or seize any property that constitutes evidence of a criminal offense in violation of the laws of the United States," and permitting delayed notice of a search in some circumstances). In general, statutes in Title 18 of the U.S. Code governing searches and seizures in criminal cases incorporate relevant sections of Federal Rule of Criminal Procedure 41 by reference. *See, e.g.*, 18 U.S.C. § 3103 (incorporating the grounds for which a search warrant may be issued). However, some provisions add statutory requirements. *See, e.g.*, 18 U.S.C. § 3109 (adding procedures for breaking doors or windows to execute a search warrant).

[42] United States v. Williams, 504 U.S. 36, 48 (1992).

[43] For example, administrative subpoenas are available for use in the investigation by the Drug Enforcement Administration; by federal agency inspectors general; and in health care fraud, child abuse, and presidential protection investigations. *See* 21 U.S.C. § 876; 5 U.S.C. App. (III) § 6; 18 U.S.C. § 3486.

[44] Subpoena authorities are unlikely to substitute for authorities applicable in national security investigations. For administrative subpoenas, one reason is that relevant statutes do not impose a gag order component; thus, national security information might be compromised. More importantly, national security investigations and the type of investigations in which such subpoenas may be used will only rarely coincide. However, criminal investigations in which grand jury subpoenas are sought may intersect with foreign intelligence investigations under FISA in situations involving criminal conduct that also has national security implications, such as international terrorism or espionage.

[45] See CRS Report 98-326, *Privacy: An Overview of Federal Statutes Governing Wiretapping and Electronic Eavesdropping*, by Gina Stevens and Charles Doyle, for a more detailed discussion of the federal laws governing wiretapping and electronic eavesdropping, along with appendices including copies of the texts of ECPA and FISA.

[46] 18 U.S.C. §§ 2510-2522.

[47] 18 U.S.C. §§ 2701-2712.

[48] 18 U.S.C. §§ 3121-3127. Pen registers capture the numbers dialed on a telephone line; trap and trace devices identify the originating number of a call on a particular phone line. *See* 18 U.S.C. § 3127(3)-(4).

[49] 18 U.S.C. § 2511.

[50] 18 U.S.C. §§ 2516, 2518(3).

[51] 18 U.S.C. § 2517.

[52] 18 U.S.C. § 2518(8).

[53] 18 U.S.C. § 2511(2)(f). FISA defines electronic surveillance to include more than the interception of wire, oral, or electronic communications, 50 U.S.C. § 1801(f), but places limitations on its definition based upon the location or identity of some or all of the parties to the communications involved.

[54] Berger v. New York, 388 U.S. 41 (1967); Katz v. United States, 389 U.S. 347 (1967); S. Rept. 90-1097, at 66 (1967).

[55] Smith v. Maryland, 442 U.S. 735 (1979); United States v. Miller, 425 U.S. 435 (1976); S. Rept. 99-541, at 3 (1986).

[56] 18 U.S.C. § 2503. But communications held by electronic communications providers for less than 180 days require a warrant, 18 U.S.C. § 2703(a).

[57] 18 U.S.C. § 2702.

[58] 18 U.S.C. §§ 2517, 2518(8).

[59] *See* 50 U.S.C. § 1801(a) (definition of "foreign power").

[60] For example, it extends to the collection of information necessary for the conduct of foreign affairs. *See* 50 U.S.C. § 1801(e) (definition of "foreign intelligence information").

[61] For example, FISA provides for emergency authorization of electronic surveillance or a physical search by the Attorney General in some circumstances, while an order is sought. 50 U.S.C. §§ 1805(e) and 1824(e), respectively. It also allows physical searches to be conducted in absence of a court order for periods of up to one year where the target is a foreign nation or component of a foreign nation, a faction of a foreign nation or nations not substantially composed of U.S. persons, or an entity openly acknowledged by a foreign government or governments to be directed and controlled by such government or governments, as long as the Attorney General: (1) certifies that the physical search is directed solely at a foreign power, there is no substantial likelihood that the search will "involve the premises, information, material, or property of a United States person," and proposed minimization procedures meet specified standards; and (2) fulfills various reporting requirements regarding minimization procedures. 50 U.S.C. § 1822. *See also* 50 U.S.C. § 1802 (electronic surveillance of such foreign powers for up to one year without a court order).

[62] 50 U.S.C. §§ 1801-1808. FISA authorizes electronic surveillance without a FISA order in specified instances involving communications between foreign powers. 50 U.S.C. § 1802.

[63] 50 U.S.C. §§ 1822-1826.

[64] 50 U.S.C. §§ 1841-1846.

[65] 50 U.S.C. §§ 1861-1862.

[66] 50 U.S.C. §§ 1881b, 1881c. As discussed *infra*, FISA also currently includes a statutory framework for targeting non-U.S. persons abroad to acquire foreign intelligence information pursuant to a joint Attorney General/Director of National Intelligence (DNI) authorization in specified circumstances. 50 U.S.C. § 1881a.

[67] 50 U.S.C. § 1804(a)(4).

[68] 50 U.S.C. §§ 1804(a)(2); 1805(c)(1)(A) and (B).

[69] 50 U.S.C. § 1805(a)(3).

[70] 50 U.S.C. § 1804(a)(7)(C) and (E).

[71] *Id.* at § 1804(a)(5). Minimization procedures, examined in greater detail *infra*, are safeguards which limit the government's use of collected information.

[72] 50 U.S.C. § 1823(a).

[73] The exceptions authorize: (1) emergency authorization by the Attorney General for up to 48 hours, if specified criteria are met, while an application for a FISC order is pursued; and (2) the installation and use of pen registers and trap and trace devices for up to 15 calendar days following a congressional declaration of war). 50 U.S.C. §§ 1843, 1844.

[74] 50 U.S.C. § 1842(c).

[75] 50 U.S.C. § 1861(b)(2).

[76] 50 U.S.C. §§ 1861-1862.

[77] *See, e.g.*, 50 U.S.C. §§ 1805(a)(2)(A) (electronic surveillance), 1824(a)(2)(A) (physical searches),1842(c) (pen register or trap and trace device).

[78] The NSL statutes are: 18 U.S.C. § 2709 of ECPA; section 1114(a)(5) of the Right to Financial Privacy Act (12 U.S.C. § 3414(a)(5)); sections 626 and 627 of the Fair Credit Reporting Act (15 U.S.C. §§1681u and 1681v); and section 802 of the National Security Act of 1947 (50 U.S.C. § 436). For a more detailed discussion of the NSL statutes and the proposals to amend them see, CRS Report RL33320, *National Security Letters in Foreign Intelligence Investigations: Legal Background and Recent Amendments*, by Charles Doyle, and CRS Report R40887, *National Security Letters: Proposed Amendments in the 111th Congress*, by Charles Doyle.

[79] According to reports by the Department of Justice Inspector General's Office, the FBI issued 39,346 NSL requests in 2003, 56,507 in 2004, 47,221 in 2005, and 49,425 in 2006. Office of the Inspector General, U.S. Department of Justice, *A Review of the Federal Bureau of Investigation's Use of National Security Letters* (March 2008) at 110.

[80] The Justice Department reported that the FISA court issued 13 tangible item orders in 2008 and 17 in 2007, *Letters* dated May 14, 2009 from Ass't Att'y Gen. Ronald Weich to Vice-

President Biden, Senators Reid and McConnell, Speaker Pelosi, and Congressmen Hoyer and Boehner, http://www.justice.gov/nsd/foia/reading_room/2008fisa-ltr.pdf.

[81] 50 U.S.C. § 436.

[82] 15 U.S.C. § 1681v.

[83] 18 U.S.C. § 2709.

[84] 15 U.S.C. § 1681u.

[85] 12 U.S.C. § 3414(a)(5).

[86] The terms "nondisclosure requirements," "secrecy requirements," and "gag orders" are used interchangeably throughout this report.

[87] 18 U.S.C. § 3511; John Doe, Inc. v. Mukasey, 549 F.3d 861 (2d Cir. 2008). *See also* discussion regarding judicial oversight, *infra*.

[88] Expansions were also made to some related authorities. For example, the USA PATRIOT Act and subsequent legislation amended the grand jury secrecy rule to permit prosecutors to disclose grand jury information to federal, state, local, or foreign law enforcement or intelligence officials under certain circumstances.

[89] 50 U.S.C. § 1804(a)(7)(B) (electronic surveillance); 50 U.S.C. § 1823(a)(7)(B) (physical searches).

[90] 50 U.S.C. § 1806(k)(1) (electronic surveillance); 50 U.S.C. § 1825 (physical searches).

[91] *Id.* at § 6001(a); 50 U.S.C. § 1801(b)(1)(C).

[92] *But see* Letter from Assistant Attorney General Ronald Weich to Hon. Patrick J. Leahy, at 5 (Sept. 14, 2009), http://judiciary.senate.gov/resources/documents/111thCongress/upload/091409WeichtoLeahy.pdf (indicating that the lone wolf provision has not yet been relied upon in a federal investigation). For more information regarding the lone wolf provision and the other expiring amendments to FISA, see CRS Report R40138, *Amendments to the Foreign Intelligence Surveillance Act (FISA) Set to Expire February 28, 2011*, by Anna C. Henning and Edward C. Liu.

[93] *See* discussion regarding the aftermath of the Terrorist Surveillance Program.

[94] The Protect America Act of 2007, P.L. 110-55.

[95] *Id.*

[96] The FISA Amendments Act of 2008, P.L. 110-261.

[97] *See, e.g.*, P.L. 109-177, § 106(b), 50 U.S.C. §§ 1861-1863; P.L. 107-56, § 505(a)(3), 18 U.S.C. § 2709.

[98] P.L. 107-56, §§ 201, 202, 18 U.S.C. § 2516(1).

[99] P.L. 107-56, § 203(b), 18 U.S.C. §§ 2510(19), 2517(1).

[100] P.L. 107-56, § 223(a), 18 U.S.C. § 2520(f).

[101] P.L. 107-56, § 217, 18 U.S.C. §§ 2511(2)(i), 2510(21).

[102] P.L. 107-56, § 209, 18 U.S.C. §§ 2703, 2510(14).

[103] P.L. 107-56, § 220, 18 U.S.C. §§ 2711, 2703.

[104] P.L. 107-56, § 212, 18 U.S.C. § 2702.

[105] 50 U.S.C. § 1805(c)(2)(B).

[106] *Id.*

[107] P.L. 107-56, § 207, 50 U.S.C. § 1805(e).

[108] P.L. 107-56, § 225, 50 U.S.C. § 1805(i). This section was expanded by section 314(a)(2)(D) of the Intelligence Authorization Act for Fiscal Year 2002, P.L. 107-108, to cover those who provide such assistance in connection with a FISA order authorizing a physical search or emergency assistance.

[109] The definition of "physical search" in FISA incorporates the standard—"reasonable expectation of privacy"—which typically triggers the Fourth Amendment warrant requirement in criminal investigations. *See* 50 U.S.C. § 1821(5) (defining "physical search" as: "any physical intrusion within the United States into premises or property (including examination of the interior of property by technical means) that is intended to result in a seizure, reproduction, inspection, or alteration of information, material, or property, *under*

circumstances in which a person has a reasonable expectation of privacy and a warrant would be required for law enforcement purposes, but does not include (A) "electronic surveillance" ... or (B) the acquisition by the United States Government of foreign intelligence information from international or foreign communications, or foreign intelligence activities conducted in accordance with otherwise applicable Federal law ....") (emphasis added).

[110] P.L. 107-56, §207, 50 U.S.C. § 1824(d). The maximum duration of a physical search order targeting a foreign power was and is one year.

[111] *Id.*

[112] P.L. 107-56, §214, 50 U.S.C. § 1842(a)(1).

[113] *Id.*

[114] P.L. 107-56, §216, 18 U.S.C. § 3123(a).

[115] 18 U.S.C. §§ 3121, 3123.

[116] P.L. 107-56, §§ 328(g), 505.

[117] *See, e.g.,* 18 U.S.C. § 2709 (2000 ed.). A textual comparison of the NSL statutes now and prior to the USA PATRIOT Act appears as an appendix in CRS Report R40887, *National Security Letters: Proposed Amendments in the 111th Congress*, by Charles Doyle.

[118] *See, e.g,,* 18 U.S.C. § 2709.

[119] Office of the Inspector General, U.S. Department of Justice, *A Review of the Federal Bureau of Investigation's Use of National Security Letters* (March 2007) (*IG Rept. I*) at 43-5; Office of the Inspector General, U.S. Department of Justice, *A Review of the Federal Bureau of Investigation's Use of National Security Letters* (March 2008) (*IG Rept. II*) at 114-16.

[120] *IG Rept. I* at 46.

[121] *Id.* at 124. Second IG's report indicated it was too soon to tell whether the FBI had eliminated the problems identified in the first report, *IG Rept. II* at 161.

[122] 50 U.S.C. §§ 1861-1862 (2000 ed.).

[123] 50 U.S.C. § 1861(a)(1).

[124] 50 U.S.C. §§ 1861-1863.

[125] 50 U.S.C. § 1861(a).

[126] P.L. 109-177, §§ 102(b), 106A.

[127] Office of the Inspector General, U.S. Department of Justice, *A Review of the Federal Bureau of Investigation's Use of Section 215 Orders for Business Records* (March 2007) (*IG 215 Rept. I*); Office of the Inspector General, U.S. Department of Justice, *A Review of the Federal Bureau of Investigation's Use of Section 215 Orders for Business Records in 2006* (March 2008) (*IG 215 Rept. II*).

[128] *IG 215 Rept.I* at 16-7.

[129] *Id.* at 17; 50 U.S.C. § 1842(d)(2)(C).

[130] *IG 215 Rept. I* at 17; *IG 215 Rept. II* at 15.

[131] *IG 215 Rept. II* at 57.

[132] *Id.*

[133] *Id.* at 58.

[134] 50 U.S.C. § 1861(b) (2000 ed., Supp. I).

[135] 50 U.S.C. § 1861(b).

[136] 50 U.S.C. § 1861(b)(2).

[137] Fed. R. Crim. P. 41(f).

[138] 18 U.S.C. § 3103a(b).

[139] See United States v. Pangburn, 983 F.2d 449 (2d Cir. 1993); United States v. Freitas, 800 F.2d 1451 (9th Cir. 1986); United States v. Simmons, 206 F.3d 392 (4th Cir. 2000).

[140] 18 U.S.C. §§ 3103a(b), 2705(b). In other Fourth Amendment cases, the Supreme Court has identified the destruction of evidence, threats to individual safety, and risk of the suspect's flight as among the permissible exigent circumstances justify delayed notice. *See, e.g.,* Wilson v. Arkansas, 514 U.S. 927, 936 (1995).

[141] Administrative Office of the United States Courts, *Report of the Director of the Administrative Office of the United States Courts on Applications for Delayed-Notice Search Warrants and Extensions*, EC-2350, 155 Cong. Rec. S7555 (daily ed. July 15, 2009) at 1-2.
[142] *Id.* at 6.
[143] P.L. 108-458, § 6002, 50 U.S.C. 1801 note.
[144] P.L. 109-177, § 114, 18 U.S.C. § 3103a(d)(1).
[145] *Id.*
[146] P.L. 109-177, § 109(a), 50 U.S.C. § 1826.
[147] P.L. 109-177, § 128(b), 50 U.S.C. § 1846(a).
[148] P.L. 107-56, § 216, 18 U.S.C. § 3123(a)(3).
[149] P.L. 107-56, § 223(c), 18 U.S.C. §§ 2510(19), 2712.
[150] 549 F.3d 861 (2d. Cir. 2008).
[151] For national security letters, such consequences include danger to the national security or to individual safety, or interference with diplomatic relations or with a criminal counter-intelligence, or counter-terrorism investigation. In a criminal context, disclosure of an officer's purpose to execute a warrant may be excused if disclosure is likely to result in adverse consequences such as the loss of evidence, flight of a suspect, or a danger to individual safety, Wilson v. Arkansas, 514 U.S. 927, 935-36 (1995).
[152] *Mukasey*, 549 F.3d at 883.
[153] 50 U.S.C. § 1861(f).
[154] 50 U.S.C. § 1861(f)(2).
[155] 549 F.3d 861, 882-83 (2d Cir. 2008) ("the fiat of a governmental official, though senior in rank and doubtless honorable in the execution of official duties, cannot displace the judicial obligation to enforce constitutional requirements").
[156] 50 U.S.C. § 1861(f)(2)(C)(ii).
[157] 50 U.S.C. § 1861(f)(2)(C)(iii).
[158] *Cf.*, 18 U.S.C. §§ 401, 402.
[159] 18 U.S.C. § 2518(5).
[160] 50 U.S.C. § 1801(h).
[161] 50 U.S.C. §§ 1806, 1825.
[162] 18 U.S.C. §§ 2517, 2518(8).
[163] 18 U.S.C. § 2709(d); 12 U.S.C. § 3414(a)(5)(B); 15 U.S.C. § 1681u(f); 50 U.S.C. § 436(e).
[164] P.L. 109-177, § 119(f).
[165] *IG Rept. II* at 64-72.
[166] *Reauthorizing the USA Patriot Act: Hearings Before the Senate Comm. on the Judiciary*, 111th Cong. (2009) (statement of U.S. Department of Justice Inspector General Glenn A. Fine).
[167] *Id.*
[168] 50 U.S.C. § 1861(g).
[169] *IG 215 Rept. II* at 76.
[170] *Id.* at 87.
[171] *See* Fed. R. Crim. P. 41(c); 18 U.S.C. § 2518(3).
[172] *See, e.g.*, 50 U.S.C. § 1804(a)(7)(B) (2008). Prior to 2001, the statute had required that "the purpose" of a FISA warrant be foreign intelligence collection.
[173] 50 U.S.C. § 1805(a)(2)(A) and (B) (electronic surveillance); 50 U.S.C. § 1824(a)(2) (physical search). In contrast, federal criminal search warrants require probable cause to believe that instrumentalities, evidence, or fruits of a crime will be found in the place to be searched. *See* Fed. R. Crim. P. 41(c).
[174] 18 U.S.C. § 32 (destruction aircraft or aircraft facilities); 18 U.S.C. § 2332a (use of weapons of mass destruction)
[175] 18 U.S.C. § 2339B (providing material support); 18 U.S.C. § 2339D (military training). While section 2339B covers attempted violations, section 2339D does not.
[176] 18 U.S.C. §§ 1961-1962 (racketeering); 18 U.S.C. § 3286 (statute of limitations).

[177] 18 U.S.C. § 2332b(g)(5) classifies over forty federal offenses as "federal crimes of terrorism."

[178] 18 U.S.C. § 2339A.

[179] 18 U.S.C. § 2339B. Neither section explicitly covers material support of the families of terrorist suicide bombers.

[180] 18 U.S.C. § 2339B(a)(1).

[181] More precisely, it requires that it had been designated or that the organization has or is engaged in terrorist activity as defined in 8 U.S.C. § 1182(a)(3)(B), or in terrorism as defined in 22 U.S.C. § 2656f(d)(2).

[182] Humanitarian Law Project v. Mukasey, 552 F.3d 916, 927 (9th Cir. 2009), *cert. granted,* ____ S.Ct. ____ (Sept. 30, 2009); United States v. Warsame, 537 F.3d 1005, 1021-22 (D. Minn. 2008).

[183] Humanitarian Law Project v. Mukasey, 552 F.3d 916, 928-30 (9th Cir. 2009), *cert. granted,* ____ S.Ct. ____ (Sept. 30, 2009).

[184] Humanitarian Law Project v. Holder (Doc. No. 08-1498), ____ S.Ct. ____ (Sept. 30, 2009); Holder v. Humanitarian Law Project (Doc. No. 09-89), ____ S.Ct. ____ (Sept. 30, 2009).

[185] 18 U.S.C. § 2283 (transportation of explosives or weapons of mass destruction knowing they are intended to be used commit a federal crime of terrorism) and § 2284 (transportation of a terrorist who intends to commit, or is in flight following commission of, a federal crime of terrorism).

[186] 20 U.S.C. §§ 1232g(j), 9573(e) (court orders for access to confidential educational records).

[187] U.S.S.G. § 3A1.4.

[188] 18 U.S.C. § 226.

[189] 20 U.S.C. § 1232g(j), § 9573(e) (court orders for access to confidential educational records).

[190] *E.g.*, 18 U.S.C. § 1001 (false statements), § 1028 (fraud relating to identification documents), § 1505 (obstruction of administrative proceedings).

[191] 18 U.S.C. § 2332b(g)(5) consists of two elements: a terrorism element ("an offense that is calculated to influence or affect the conduct of government by intimidation or coercion, or to retaliate against government conduct," 18 U.S.C. § 2332b(g)(5)(A)) and one listing specific federal crimes ("an offense that ... is a violation of [specified sections]," 18 U.S.C. § 2332b(g)(5)(B)). Most statutes cross reference only to section 2332b(g)(5)(B).

[192] *See* 18 U.S.C. § 2331(1) (defining "international terrorism"); 18 U.S.C. § 2331(5) (defining "domestic terrorism").

[193] P.L. 107-56, § 802.

[194] *See e.g., How the USA PATRIOT Act Will permit Governmental Infringement upon the Privacy of Americans in the Name of "Intelligence" Investigations*, 150 U. Pa. L. Rev. 1651, 1688-692 (2002).

[195] James Risen and Eric Lichtblau, *Bush Lets U.S. Spy on Callers Without Courts*, N.Y. Times, Dec. 16, 2005, at 1.

[196] U.S. Department of Justice, *Legal Authorities Supporting the Activities of the National Security Agency Described by the President*, at 5, 17, Jan. 19, 2006, http://www.usdoj.gov/opa/whitepaperonnsalegalauthorities.pdf. *See also* CRS Report R40888, *Presidential Authority to Conduct Warrantless Electronic Surveillance to Gather Foreign Intelligence Information*, by Elizabeth B. Bazan and Jennifer K. Elsea.

[197] The "procedures in [Title III of the Omnibus Crime Control and Safe Streets Act] and the Foreign Intelligence Surveillance Act of 1978 shall be *the exclusive means* by which electronic surveillance, as defined in section 101 of FISA, and the interception of domestic wire, oral, and electronic communications may be conducted." 18 U.S.C. § 2511(2)(f) (emphasis added).

[198] S.Rept. 110-209, at 4. *See also* Letter from Attorney General Gonzales to Senate Judiciary Committee Chairman Patrick Leahy and Senator Arlen Specter (January 17, 2007).

[199] *Id.* at 7.

[200] United States v. Reynolds, 345 U.S. 1, 10 (1953).

[201] Hepting v. AT&T, 439 F. Supp. 2d 974, 994 (N.D. Cal. 2006).

[202] 50 U.S.C. § 1885a.

[203] Alternatively, the Attorney General can certify that the alleged assistance was not in fact provided by the defendant. 50 U.S.C. § 1885a(a)(5).

[204] *See* Public Certification of the Attorney General of the U.S., In re Nat'l Security Telecommunications Records Litigation, MDL Dkt. No. 06-1791-VRW (N.D. Cal. Sep. 19, 2008) (on file with author).

[205] In re NSA Telcoms. Records Litig., 633 F. Supp. 2d 949 (N.D. Cal. 2009).

[206] Chase Sec. Corp. v. Donaldson, 325 U.S. 304, 315-316 (1945) (noting in dicta that "some rules of law probably could not be changed retroactively without hardship and oppression" to the extent that it would be considered a violation of the Due Process Clause).

[207] See Plaut v. Spendthrift Farm, Inc., 514 U.S. 211 (1995) (federal law that reopened final judgment in cases where statute of limitations barred claim was a violation of the separation of powers).

[208] P.L. 110-55, 50 U.S.C. §§ 1805a-1805c.

[209] P.L. 110-261, § 101, 50 U.S.C. §§ 1881-1881g.

[210] 50 U.S.C. § 1881a.

[211] 50 U.S.C. § 1881a(b)(2).

[212] 50 U.S.C. §§ 1881b and 1881c.

[213] Letter from the U.S. Department of Justice to Hon. Patrick J. Leahy (Sept. 14, 2009), http://judiciary.

[214] *Id.*

[215] *See e.g., Restoring the Rule of Law: Hearing Before the Senate Comm. on the Judiciary, Subcomm. on the Constitution*, 110th Cong. (Sept. 16, 2008) (statement of Suzanne E. Spaulding, Esq.).

[216] *Unchecked National Security Letter Powers and Our Civil Liberties: Hearing Before the House Perm. Select Comm. on Intelligence*, 110th Cong. (Mar. 28, 2007) (statement of Lisa Graves, then Deputy Director, Center for National Security Studies).

In: Government Access and Collection of Private... ISBN: 978-1-60876-085-5
Editors: Corey D. Heims

Chapter 3

STATEMENT OF GLENN A. FINE, INSPECTOR GENERAL, U.S. DEPARTMENT OF JUSTICE, BEFORE THE SENATE COMMITTEE ON THE JUDICIARY, "REAUTHORIZING THE USA PATRIOT ACT"

Glenn A. Fine

Mr. Chairman, Ranking Member Sessions, and Members of the Judiciary Committee:

Thank you for inviting me to testify about the Office of the Inspector General's (OIG) oversight work related to reauthorization of the USA Patriot Act. Our most significant oversight work regarding the Patriot Act has focused on the Federal Bureau of Investigation's (FBI) use of national security letters (NSL) and Section 215 orders to obtain business records, and I will focus primarily on those issues in my testimony today.

In 2005, the Patriot Reauthorization Act directed the OIG to review the FBI's use of NSLs and Section 215 orders. In March 2007, the OIG issued reports examining the FBI's use of Section 215 orders and NSLs, which found serious misuse of NSL authorities. By contrast, the authors found that Section 215 orders generally were not subject to misuse, although they were used much less frequently than NSLs. A second set of reports, issued in March 2008, again examined the use of Section 215 orders and NLS, including the measures taken or proposed by the FBI and the Department of Justice (Department) to address the OIG's recommendations regarding the misuse of NSLs.

In this written statement, I first summarize the findings of our NSL and Section 215 reports. I also provide an update on the status of the OIG's ongoing review of the FBI's previous use of so-called "exigent letters" rather than NSLs to obtain telephone records. I then discuss the actions the FBI and the Department have taken in response to our recommendations, including the FBI's creation of an Office of Integrity and Compliance and oversight of the FBI's use of NSLs by the Department's National Security Division.

Finally, I briefly discuss other OIG work related to the Patriot Act, including the OIG's responsibilities under Section 1001 of the Patriot Act to examine allegations of civil rights and civil liberties complaints against Department employees. I also note several ongoing and recently completed OIG reviews that, while not directly related to the Patriot Act, affect the FBI's ability to perform its important mission.

I. Summary of Findings of OIG Reports on the FBI's Use of National Security Letters from 2003 – 2006

As required by the Patriot Reauthorization Act, the OIG examined the FBI's use of NSLs from 2003 to 2006. As discussed in our two reports, the FBI is authorized under five statutory provisions to use NSLs to obtain records such as telephone toll billing records and subscriber information from communication service providers, transactional records from Internet service providers, bank records from financial institutions, and consumer credit information from credit reporting agencies.

The original Patriot Act in 2001 significantly broadened the FBI's authority to use NSLs by both lowering the threshold standard for issuing them and by expanding the number of FBI officials who could sign the letters. First, the Patriot Act eliminated the requirement that the information sought must pertain to a foreign power or an agent of a foreign power. Instead, it substituted the lower threshold standard that the information requested must be relevant to or sought for an investigation to protect against international terrorism or espionage. In addition, the Patriot Act permitted Special Agents in Charge (SAC) of the FBI's 56 field offices to sign national security letters, which significantly expanded approval authority beyond the previously limited number of FBI Headquarters officials. The Patriot Act also added a new authority allowing NSLs to be used to obtain consumer full credit reports in international terrorism investigations.

Our NSL reports examined the effectiveness of NSLs, which are used by the FBI for various purposes, including developing evidence to support applications for orders issued under the *Foreign Intelligence Surveillance Act* (FISA), developing links between subjects of FBI investigations and other individuals, providing leads and evidence to allow FBI agents to initiate or close investigations, and corroborating information obtained by other investigative techniques. During both of our NSL reviews, FBI personnel told us that they believe NSLs are indispensable investigative tools in many counterterrorism and counterintelligence investigations.

Our review of the FBI's use of NSLs from 2003 – 2006 identified a general upward trend in their use, with the FBI issuing more than 192,000 NSL requests during this 4-year period.

However, the OIG found that these statistics, which were based on information from the FBI's database, significantly understated the total number of NSL requests issued by the FBI because the FBI's tracking database was inaccurate and did not include all NSL requests. For example, our examination of case files at four FBI field offices found approximately 22 percent more NSL requests in the case files that we examined than were recorded in the database for those same files.

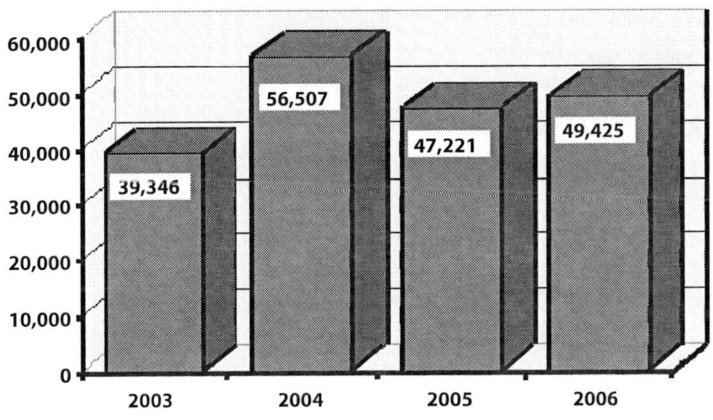

National Security Letter Requests (2003 through 2006)

Our reports recognized the significant challenges the FBI faced and the major organizational changes it was undergoing during our review period. Nevertheless, we concluded that the FBI engaged in serious misuse of NSL authorities. For example, from 2003 to 2005 the FBI identified 26 possible intelligence violations involving its use of NSLs. The possible violations included issuing NSLs without proper authorization and making improper requests under the statutes cited in the NSLs.

However, in addition to the possible violations reported by the FBI, we conducted an independent review of FBI case files in four field offices to determine if there were unreported violations of NSL authorities, Attorney General Guidelines, or internal FBI policies governing the approval and use of NSLs. Our review of 293 national security letters in 77 files found 22 possible violations that had not been identified or reported by the FBI. The violations we found fell into three categories: improper authorization for the NSL, improper requests under the pertinent national security letter statutes, and unauthorized collections.

Examples of the violations we identified included issuing NSLs for consumer full credit reports in a counterintelligence case, which is not statutorily permitted; issuing an NSL for a consumer full credit report when the FBI Special Agent in Charge had approved an NSL for more limited credit information under a different NSL authority; issuing an NSL when the investigation had lapsed; and obtaining telephone toll billing records for periods in excess of the time period requested in the NSL due to third-party errors.

Thus, it is significant that in the limited file review we conducted of 77 investigative files in 4 FBI field offices, we identified nearly as many NSL-related violations (22) as the total number of possible violations that the FBI had identified (26) in reports from all FBI Headquarters and field divisions over the 3-year period. Moreover, 17 of the 77 files we reviewed (22 percent) had 1 or more violations.

Most troubling, the OIG's March 2007 review also identified more than 700 instances in which the FBI improperly obtained telephone toll billing records and subscriber information from communication service providers by issuing so-called "exigent letters" signed by personnel in the FBI's Counterterrorism Division rather than by issuing proper NSLs. These exigent letters stated they were being issued due to exigent circumstances and the FBI was in the process of obtaining subpoenas for the requested information. However, the OIG found that in some instances there was no pending investigation associated with the request at the time the exigent letters were sent; many were not issued in exigent circumstances; the FBI was unable to determine which letters were sent in exigent circumstances due to inadequate recordkeeping; and subpoenas in many instances had not, in fact, been submitted to the U.S. Attorneys Offices as represented in the exigent letters. As a result of our review, the FBI ended its practice of using exigent letters. As I discuss in more detail later in this statement, the OIG is in the final stages of our review that assesses who was responsible for the misuse of exigent letters and other improper requests for telephone records.

The OIG's March 2007 report on NSLs made 10 recommendations to the FBI, including improving its database to ensure that it captures timely, complete, and accurate data on NSLs; issuing additional guidance to field offices to assist in identifying possible intelligence violations arising from the use of NSLs; and taking steps to ensure that it employs NSLs in accordance with the requirements of NSL authorities, Department guidelines, and internal policy. The FBI concurred with all of our recommendations and agreed to implement corrective actions.

One year later, in March 2008, the OIG issued a follow-up review on the FBI's use of NSLs in which we determined that the FBI and the Department had made significant progress implementing recommendations from our first report and adopting corrective actions to address the serious problems we identified. The measures implemented by the FBI included developing a new NSL data system designed to facilitate the issuance and tracking of NSLs and ensure accurate reports to Congress and the public on NSL usage; issuing NSL guidance memoranda and conducting training of field and headquarters personnel; and creating a new FBI Office of Integrity and Compliance, an internal oversight office modeled after private sector compliance programs.

We also found that the FBI had devoted substantial time and resources to ensure that its field managers and agents understood the seriousness of the FBI's shortcomings in its use of NSLs and their responsibility for correcting these deficiencies. In addition, in response to our March 2007 findings the Department's National Security Division instituted periodic national security reviews of FBI field and Headquarters divisions to assess whether the FBI was using various intelligence techniques, including NSLs, in accordance with applicable laws, guidelines, and policies.

Our March 2008 report also examined whether NSLs issued after the effective date of the Patriot Reauthorization Act contained the required certifications to impose non-disclosure and confidentially requirements on NSL recipients. In the random sample of NSLs we reviewed, we found that 97percent of the NSLs imposed non-disclosure and confidentiality requirements and almost all contained the required certifications. We found that some of the justifications for imposing this requirement were perfunctory and conclusory, and that a small number of the NSL approval memoranda failed to comply with internal FBI policy.

Our March 2008 report made 17 additional recommendations to improve the FBI's use and oversight of NSLs, such as providing additional guidance and training for FBI agents on the proper use of NSLs and on the reviewing, filing, and retention of NSL-derived information; reinforcing the need for FBI agents and supervisors to determine whether there is adequate justification for imposing non-disclosure and confidentiality requirements on NSL recipients; regularly monitoring the preparation and handling of NSLs; and providing timely reports of possible intelligence violations to FBI Headquarters. The FBI agreed with the recommendations and said it would implement additional actions to address our findings.

II. Summary of Findings of OIG Reports on the FBI's Use of Section 215 Requests for Business Records from 2002 – 2006

As also directed by the 2005 Patriot Reauthorization Act, the OIG issued two reports on the FBI's use of Section 215 orders to obtain business records. Section 215 of the Patriot Act allows the FBI to seek an order from the Foreign Intelligence Surveillance Court to obtain "any tangible thing," including books, records, and other items from any business, organization, or entity if the item is for an authorized investigation to protect against international terrorism or clandestine intelligence activity. This is one of the three provisions that "sunsets" in December 2009 and is a focus of this hearing.

Our first report on the use of Section 215 orders, issued in March 2007, examined the FBI's use of Section 215 authority from 2002 through 2005. We found that the Department's Office of Intelligence Policy and Review, on behalf of the FBI, submitted requests for two different types of Section 215 applications to the FISA Court: "pure" Section 215 applications and "combination" Section 215 applications. A "pure" Section 215 application referred to a Section 215 application for any tangible item that was not associated with any other FISA authority. A "combination" Section 215 application referred to a Section 215 request that was added to a FISA application for pen register/trap and trace orders, which identify incoming and outgoing telephone numbers called on a particular line.

We found that from 2002 through 2005 the Department, on behalf of the FBI, submitted to the FISA Court a total of 21 pure Section 215 applications and 141 combination Section 215 applications. We found only two instances involving improper use of these Section 215 orders, which involved overcollections in response to Section 215 combination pen/register trap and trace orders. In both instances, the FBI identified the overcollections and reported the matter to the FISA Court and the Intelligence Oversight Board (IOB).

Our report also found that the FBI has not used Section 215 orders as effectively as it could have because of legal, bureaucratic, or other impediments to obtaining these orders. For example, we found significant delays within the FBI and the Department in processing requests for Section 215 orders. We also determined through our interviews that FBI field offices did not fully understand Section 215 orders or the process for obtaining them.

Our follow-up report issued in March 2008 examined the FBI's use of Section 215 orders in 2006. We found that in 2006 the FBI and the Department processed 15 "pure" Section 215 applications and 32 "combination" Section 215 applications that were formally submitted to and approved by the FISA Court. Six additional 215 applications were withdrawn by the FBI before they were formally submitted to the FISA Court.

In both of our reports, we found no instance in which the information obtained from a Section 215 order resulted in a major case development. However, FBI personnel said that the importance of information from Section 215 orders is sometimes not known until much later in an investigation – for example, when the information was linked to some other piece of intelligence. We also found that little of the information obtained through Section 215 orders had been disseminated to intelligence agencies outside the Department. Nevertheless, FBI personnel told us that Section 215 authority was essential to national security investigations because it was the only compulsory process for certain kinds of records that could not be obtained through alternative means, such as NSLs or grand jury subpoenas.

Our March 2008 review did not identify any illegal use of Section 215 orders in 2006. However, we found two instances when the FBI received more information than it requested in the Section 215 orders. In one case, approximately 2 months passed before the FBI recognized it was receiving additional information that was beyond the scope of the FISA Court order. The FBI reported this incident to the IOB, and the additional information was sequestered with the FISA Court. In the other case, the FBI quickly determined that it inadvertently received information not authorized by the Section 215 order and isolated the records. However, the FBI concluded that the matter was not reportable to the IOB and that it should be able to use the material as if it were "voluntarily produced" because the information was not statutorily protected. We disagreed with this conclusion, and our report recommended that the FBI develop procedures for identifying and handling information that is produced in response to, but outside the scope of, Section 215 orders.

In addition, our report discussed another case in which the FISA Court twice refused to authorize a Section 215 order based on concerns that the investigation was premised on protected First Amendment activity. However, the FBI subsequently issued NSLs to obtain information about the subject based on the same factual predicate and without a review to ensure the investigation did not violate the subject's First Amendment rights. We questioned the appropriateness of the FBI's actions because the NSL statute contains the same First Amendment caveat as the Section 215 statute.

Of the three recommendations we made in our 215 reports, the FBI has addressed one recommendation, partially addressed a second recommendation, and has yet to address the third.

First, we recommended that the FBI develop procedures for reviewing materials received from Section 215 orders to ensure that it has not received information not authorized by the FISA Court orders. In response, the FBI developed a policy that requires the case agent to review material produced pursuant to a Section 215 order to determine whether the materials produced were responsive to the 215 order prior to uploading the material into FBI databases.

Second, we recommended that the FBI develop procedures for handling material that is produced in response to, but outside the scope of, a Section 215 order. The FBI responded by stating that it would sequester overproduced material that is "statutorily protected." However, the FBI's policy allows agents to treat non-statutorily protected material as "voluntarily produced" without any inquiry whether the overproduced material was inadvertently or voluntarily produced.

We disagree with the FBI's position on this matter for several reasons. The collections under a Section 215 order can involve non-public information about U.S. persons who are not the subject of national security investigations, and the FBI often uploads such information into FBI databases. The FBI's comparison of a Section 215 order to a grand jury subpoena or civil discovery request is misplaced because, unlike a grand jury subpoena or civil discovery request, a Section 215 order is issued by the FISA Court. Moreover, unlike in the civil or grand jury context, it is unlikely that the persons or entities whose interests are affected by the overproduced records in response to a Section 215 order will learn that information about them has been uploaded into the FBI's databases. We also believe that the distinction that the FBI makes – between statutorily protected records and non-statutorily protected records – when a provider produces records beyond that which is called for by the Section 215 order should not be dispositive as to whether the records are uploaded into the FBI's databases. Finally, we do not believe that it is so difficult or burdensome for the FBI to inquire with the provider whether the records were produced inadvertently (which will likely be the cases in many instances) or, in the alternative, to obtain a Section 215 order for the overproduced material.

Our third recommendation related to the minimization procedures that the Patriot Reauthorization Act required the Department to implement for records obtained pursuant to Section 215 orders. The Reauthorization Act required specific procedures designed for Section 215 material that would minimize the retention and prohibit the dissemination of non-publicly available information concerning United States persons consistent with national security interests. The Reauthorization Act required that these procedures be adopted by September 5, 2006.

However, there was disagreement between the Department and the FBI regarding the definitions and scope of minimization procedures in general, including the time period for retention of Section 215 records, and whether to include procedures for addressing information received in response to but beyond the scope of the Section 215 order. To meet the statutory deadline, the Department adopted sections of the Attorney General Guidelines for FBI National Security Investigations and Foreign Intelligence Collections of October 31, 2003 (Guidelines) as "interim" minimization procedures for business records.

In our March 2008 Report, we concluded that these interim minimization procedures were deficient. The interim procedures were not specific to Section 215 records -- in fact, compliance with the Guidelines was already a prerequisite to obtaining a Section 215 order. In our report, we again recommended that the Department continue to work to develop appropriate standard minimization procedures for Section 215 records.

According to the FBI, the Department has drafted new minimization procedures for business records. However these procedures have not been issued.

III. OIG's Exigent Letter Investigation

As noted above, perhaps the most troubling finding in our review of the FBI's use of NSLs involved the use of exigent letters. In our 2007 NSL report, we found that from March 2003 to November 2006 personnel in the FBI's Communications Analysis Unit (CAU) issued at least 722 exigent letters to three communication service providers seeking telephone records. Most of the letters stated that the records were requested "due to exigent circumstances" and that grand jury subpoenas for the records had been "submitted to the U.S. Attorney's Office who will process and serve them formally. . . as expeditiously as possible."

Yet, contrary to the assertions in the exigent letters, subpoenas requesting the telephone records in many instances had not been provided to the U.S. Attorney's Office before the letters were issued. We also interviewed witnesses who told us that the FBI sometimes used exigent letters in non-emergency circumstances.

The Electronic Communications Privacy Act (ECPA) prohibits communication service providers from disclosing telephone records to the government unless compelled to do so by legal process such as an NSL, or pursuant to the voluntary emergency disclosure provision of ECPA, 18 U.S.C. Section 2702(c)(4). We concluded that the exigent letters did not constitute valid legal process under ECPA. We also were not persuaded by the FBI's justification of the letters under the emergency voluntary disclosure provision for several reasons, including that the letters were sometimes used in non-emergency circumstances and that senior FBI attorneys told us they did not rely on the emergency voluntary disclosure provision to authorize the letters at the time. We concluded that the FBI's use of exigent letters to obtain telephone records was an improper circumvention of ECPA.

After issuance of our NSL report, we conducted a separate review to examine in detail the FBI's use of exigent letters and other informal requests for telephone records, and also to determine who in the FBI was accountable for these improper uses. The OIG has completed a draft report regarding the misuse of exigent letters, as well as other informal requests such as oral and e-mail requests to the service providers for telephone records. In addition, we reviewed the FBI's issuance of after-the-fact NSLs to "cover" or validate records the FBI had received pursuant to exigent letters and other informal requests. Our report examines the accountability of FBI agents, supervisors, lawyers, and managers who used or condoned the use of these exigent letters and other informal requests for records.

In April 2009, pursuant to the OIG's normal process, we provided the FBI and the Department our draft report and asked for comments on its factual accuracy and whether any information in the report was classified or too sensitive for public release. The FBI's response was delayed, and subsequently the Office of the Director of National Intelligence (ODNI) became involved and consulted with other intelligence agencies in conducting a classification and sensitivity review. We recently received these comments from the FBI and ODNI, and we have made available an unclassified version of the report to subjects of the review for their comments. We will provide our report to the Committee and issue it publicly as soon as it is completed.

IV. Assessment of the FBI's and Department's Responses to the OIG Reports

In this section, I discuss the FBI's and the Department's responses to our NSL reports. Although we have not yet conducted another follow-up review of the FBI's response to our reports, we have been monitoring the FBI's implementation of our recommendations. For example, the OIG has met with officials from the FBI's National Security Law Branch and others staff within the FBI's Office of General Counsel and with officials in the FBI's Office of Integrity and Compliance to discuss their actions to institute corrective actions. We also have been briefed on the new NSL data management subsystem that the FBI deployed last year to address some of the problems we identified in our NSL reports. In addition, we have reviewed internal audits conducted by the FBI Inspection Division, which concluded that there has been a decrease in several types of administrative errors in the use of NSLs that we described in our reports.

We also met with officials in the Department's National Security Division who are regularly examining the FBI's performance regarding the use of NSLs in its counterterrorism and counterintelligence investigations.

In the following sections, I offer the OIG's thoughts on the FBI's and the Department's responses to the findings in our reports. In general, our sense is that the FBI is taking seriously its need to implement corrective action and to ensure that controls are implemented to prevent the serious violations our reports disclosed.

A. FBI Corrective Actions

The FBI has taken a series of actions in an effort to address our recommendations regarding NSLs. For example, in January 2008 the FBI deployed a new NSL computer subsystem built on the same computer application used to manage its Foreign Intelligence Surveillance Act (FISA) data. The NSL subsystem is now in use in all FBI field offices and at FBI Headquarters. This new system standardizes and automatically tracks NSL requests by creating mandatory fields for NSLs that must be completed by the requesting FBI case agent or official before a request to issue an NSL can be routed for review and approval by FBI supervisors, Chief Division Counsel, and Special Agents in Charge. This new process should eliminate discrepancies between NSL requests and approval documents and, among other information, also maintain a record of the U.S. person status of each target of an NSL request. While this subsystem will not eliminate all instances of noncompliance with NSL requirements, it has reduced common errors in NSLs that were identified in our reports, and it also has enhanced the FBI's ability to accurately track NSLs and compile reports to Congress and other oversight entities.

In response to our recommendations that the FBI improve guidance and training with respect to the NSL process, in December 2008 the FBI issued a comprehensive Domestic Investigations and Operations Guide. According to the FBI, this Guide is being used to provide intensive training throughout the FBI on the proper use of investigative authority in general and supplements and reinforces the more focused training on the use of NSLs already being provided.

In response to our concern that the FBI was issuing NSLs contrary to statutory limitations, AG Guidelines, or internal FBI guidance, the FBI reported that its Inspection Division will periodically review a sample of NSLs to examine whether the necessary showing of relevance is made in each cover document accompanying an NSL and whether other actions are taken in compliance with NSL authorities and FBI policies. We have been told that the Inspection Division intends to conduct such audits on a quarterly basis, although it has not yet begun to conduct these quarterly reviews.

In addition, in response to the serious violations we found in our two NSL reports the FBI created an Office of Integrity and Compliance (OIC) in 2007 which is modeled after private sector compliance programs. According to the FBI, the OIC's purpose is "to develop, implement, and oversee a program that ensures there are processes and procedures in place that promote FBI compliance with both the letter and spirit of all applicable laws, regulations, and policies." The FBI reported that the OIC will establish policies on compliance standards, guide assessments of FBI programs to determine areas at risk of non-compliance, and develop training for FBI employees that will mitigate those risks. The OIC will also work with the FBI Inspections Division to identify high-risk areas and ensure that compliance monitoring is carefully planned and executed. At present, the OIC is staffed by 15 personnel, and includes 9 attorneys, 3 program analysts, 1 administrative assistant, 1 special agent/attorney (on an 18-month detail), and 1 Assistant Director.

We believe this office can perform a valuable function by providing a process for identifying problem areas throughout the FBI, assessing existing FBI control mechanisms, and developing and implementing better internal controls on FBI procedures, including its use of NSLs. However, the OIC's responsibilities cover all operational and program areas in the FBI, and we do not believe this office should be looked to as the primary oversight mechanism to ensure proper use of NSLs and Section 215 orders.

In addition, in our March 2008 report we recommended that the FBI consider providing the OIC with a larger permanent staff. The small size of the OIC remains a concern to us because at its present strength it cannot independently conduct risk assessments of FBI's operations. Instead, the OIC relies on staff from the responsible program offices – the "risk owners" – to self-identify those areas of their operations most at risk of non-compliance with laws or regulations. We are concerned that relying on self-identification rather than aggressive independent review can result in assessments that focus on already known problems and miss unknown or emerging risks. Further, relying on program personnel to identify risks and conduct the compliance reviews puts the program personnel in the potentially difficult position of criticizing their FBI colleagues and supervisors.

Because of the importance of the OIC and the emphasis the FBI has placed on this office in addressing the problems we found in our NSL reports, the OIG intends to initiate a separate review to assess in detail the work of this office.

We also believe that additional work is needed to address other concerns we raised in our reports. For example, in our NSL reviews we recommended that the FBI consider changing the reporting structure for Chief Division Counsel (CDCs), the chief lawyers in each FBI field office. FBI Division Counsel play a critical role in reviewing and approving NSLs. Chief Division Counsel are responsible for identifying and correcting erroneous information in NSLs and NSL approval memoranda, resolving questions about the scope of the NSL statutes, ensuring adequate predication for NSL requests, and providing advice on issues concerning the collection of any unauthorized information through any national security letters.

Chief Division Counsel report to the Special Agents in Charge of the field offices in which they work, not to the Office of General Counsel (OGC) at FBI Headquarters. As a result, personnel decisions such as performance reviews, compensation, and promotion determinations concerning Chief Division Counsel are made by the Special Agents in Charge. We also found in our review that because Division Counsel report primarily to SACs rather than to FBI OGC, some Chief Division Counsel are reluctant to question NSL requests or to challenge requests generated in the course of field office investigations.

We understand that the FBI recently has taken steps to open Chief Division positions to non-agent attorneys and that other chain-of-command changes are under consideration, but at present the FBI has not modified the reporting structure for Chief Division Counsel. We believe this is a significant issue that should be addressed, and we remain concerned that Chief Division Counsel still report to and are supervised by their Special Agents in Charge, and therefore the Chief Division Counsel may not always provide the independent and rigorous review needed of the decision to approve NSLs.

B. National Security Division Corrective Actions

Our March 2008 report noted that the Department's National Security Division (NSD) has implemented additional measures to seek to ensure better compliance with NSL authorities. For example, in 2007 the NSD began reviews, modeled in part on the file reviews conducted by the OIG in our first NSL report, to examine whether the FBI is using various intelligence techniques including NSLs in accordance with applicable laws, guidelines, and policies. In conjunction with the FBI's Office of General Counsel, NSD attorneys review national security investigation files at the FBI. Among other things, the reviews examine FBI compliance with Attorney General national security investigation guidelines, use of NSLs, predication for national security investigations, and referrals to the Intelligence Oversight Board.

To date the NSD has conducted approximately 43 reviews, including 38 reviews of FBI field offices, 3 follow-up reviews of previously visited field offices, and 2 reviews of FBI Headquarters components. By the close of 2010, the NSD plans to complete reviews at all 56 FBI field offices and at FBI Headquarters.

NSD officials told us that they have observed during these reviews a significant decline in compliance issues with regard to NSLs, particularly since the FBI implemented its NSL data subsystem. However, the NSD reviews have identified areas of continuing concern, including FBI personnel not consistently following FBI guidance that material collected as a result of third party overproductions should not be uploaded into FBI databases or used to further the investigation pending review by Chief Division Counsel, and failures to specify in NSL approval documents the relevance of records sought to authorized national security investigations.

C. Department NSL Working Group

In response to the 2005 Patriot Reauthorization Act and the recommendations in our first NSL report, the Attorney General formed a Working Group (NSL Working Group) to examine how NSL-derived information is used and retained by the FBI. The Working Group was also charged with proposing minimization procedures that would ensure the FBI's collection of information through NSLs and its retention of NSL-derived information was limited to the minimum necessary to carry out its counterterrorism mission.

In August 2007, the NSL Working Group sent the Attorney General its report and proposed minimization procedures. However, we had several concerns with the findings and recommendations of the Working Group's report, which we discussed in our March 2008 NSL report. In particular, we disagreed with the Working Group about the sufficiency of existing privacy safeguards and measures for minimizing the retention of NSL-derived information. We disagreed because the controls the Working Group cited as providing safeguards predated our NSL reviews, yet we found serious abuses of the NSL authorities.

As a result, the Acting Privacy Officer decided to reconsider the recommendations and withdrew them. The Working Group has subsequently developed new recommendations for NSL minimization procedures, which are still being considered within the Department and have not yet been issued. We believe that the Department should promptly consider the Working Group's proposal and issue final minimization procedures for NSLs that address the collection of information through NSLs, how the FBI can upload NSL information in FBI databases, the dissemination of NSL information, the appropriate tagging and tracking of NSL derived information in FBI databases and files, and the time period for retention of NSL obtained information. At this point, more than 2 years have elapsed since after our first report was issued, and final guidance is needed and overdue.

V. OTHER OIG REPORTS

I also want to briefly highlight several OIG reviews that may be of interest to the Committee. In addition to requiring OIG reviews of the FBI's use of NSLs and Section 215 orders, Section 1001 of the Patriot Act directed the OIG to undertake a series of actions related to claims of civil rights or civil liberties violations allegedly committed by DOJ employees. Specifically, Section 1001 required the OIG to "review information and receive complaints alleging abuses of civil rights and civil liberties by employees and officials of the Department of Justice." It also required the OIG to provide semiannual reports to Congress on the implementation of the OIG's responsibilities under Section 1001. The OIG has issued 15 Section 1001 reports since enactment of the legislation in October 2001. These OIG reports describe the allegations of civil rights and civil liberties abuses we received during each 6-month period and how we handled them.

The OIG has also conducted numerous other reviews of the FBI that, while not directly involving Patriot Act authorities, relate to FBI programs and functions that can impact its ability to perform its vital missions. For example, the OIG is continuing a series of ongoing reviews examining the FBI's development of its Sentinel case management project. The Sentinel program is intended to upgrade the FBI's electronic case management system to improve the FBI's ability to use and share case information. Since March 2006, we have issued four audits reports that focus on the planning and development of Sentinel, the FBI's processes and controls for managing Sentinel, and the contract with Lockheed Martin to develop Sentinel. We are nearing completion of our fifth audit on these issues.

In addition, the OIG has conducted reviews of the accuracy of the FBI's terrorist watchlist and the FBI's role in connection with the President's Surveillance Program.

The OIG also is conducting a follow-up review of where the FBI has allocated its investigative resources. In the aftermath of the September 11,

2001, terrorist attacks, the FBI underwent a broad transformation aimed at focusing the agency on terrorism and intelligence-related matters. The OIG issued three previous audit reports examining how the FBI has managed this reprioritization and the impact it has had on the FBI's more traditional criminal investigations. Our current audit is examining whether the FBI has improved its process for allocating resources among its various operations and is also examining the changes in the FBI's allocation of resources during the past 3 years.

In addition, we are nearing completion of a follow-up audit of the FBI's foreign language translation program. This review is assessing the FBI's ability to translate foreign language information it receives and whether the FBI ensures the appropriate prioritization of translation work, accurate and timely translations of pertinent information, and adequate pre- and post-hire security screening of linguists. This review is also examining the FBI's success in meeting linguist hiring goals and the extent of any translation backlogs and the efforts taken by the FBI to address these backlogs.

VI. Conclusion

In sum, the Patriot Act gave the FBI significant new powers to perform its vital counterterrorism and counterintelligence missions. Our reviews found that, with regard to the use of national security letters, the FBI did not initially take seriously enough its responsibility to ensure that these letters were used in accord with the law, Attorney General Guidelines, or FBI policies. Since our disclosure of the abuses of NSLs, we believe that the FBI has devoted significant time, energy, and resources to correcting its errors, and has also attempted to ensure that its employees understand the seriousness of the FBI's shortcomings with respect to its use of national security letters and the FBI's responsibility for correcting these deficiencies.

However, this is an ongoing process and it is too early to definitively state whether the FBI's efforts have eliminated the problems we found with its use of these authorities. We also believe that as Congress considers reauthorizing provisions of the Patriot Act, it must ensure through continual and aggressive oversight that the FBI uses these important and intrusive investigative authorities appropriately. We believe this oversight should come from several different levels and from different entities – not only congressional oversight hearings, but also rigorous oversight by FBI Headquarters managers and by

FBI field supervisors, and regular oversight by the Department's National Security Division. The OIG also has an important role to play in this oversight process, and we intend to continue our reviews of the FBI's use of Patriot Act authorities, including NSLs and Section 215 orders.

That concludes my prepared statement. I would be pleased to answer any questions.

In: Government Access and Collection of Private... ISBN: 978-1-60876-085-5
Editors: Corey D. Heims

Chapter 4

STATEMENT OF LISA GRAVES[1], EXECUTIVE DIRECTOR, CENTER FOR MEDIA AND DEMOCRACY[2], BEFORE THE SENATE COMMITTEE ON THE JUDICIARY, "REFORMING THE USA PATRIOT ACT AND EXPANDED SURVEILLANCE OF AMERICANS"

Lisa Graves

Chairman Leahy, Ranking Member Sessions, and Members of the Senate Judiciary Committee, thank you for the opportunity to testify today.

I am pleased to endorse the improvements in the Patriot Act Sunset Extension Act that was introduced this week by Senator Leahy, a staunch defender of liberty and security. He was right to vote against the deeply flawed Patriot Act expansion in 2006, and his determination to begin this reform of these powers is worthy of support. These reforms are an important down-payment toward restoring liberties that have been lost. I hope these and additional reforms of federal surveillance powers that have been excessively expanded will be adopted by Congress and signed into law by President Obama.

I. These Powers Are about Us, about Who We Are as Americans

Let me begin with someone far braver and more eloquent than me, Captain Ian Fishback, a U.S. soldier in Iraq who challenged the abuse of prisoners and wrote about "the larger question that this generation will answer":

> Do we sacrifice our ideals in order to preserve security? Terrorism inspires fear and suppresses ideas like freedom and individual rights. Overcoming the fear posed by terrorist threats is a tremendous test of our courage. Will we confront danger and adversity in order to preserve our ideals, or will our courage and commitment to individual rights wither at the prospect of sacrifice? My response is simple. If we abandon our ideals in the face of adversity and aggression, then those ideals were never really in our possession. I would rather die fighting than give up even the smallest part of the idea that is "America."[3]

I agree that we must transcend the fear others want to trigger in our hearts, and we need to summon tremendous courage to help preserve and restore ideals that truly make America the land of the free.

One of the challenges in this area is whether we have the will to see beyond a particular investigation or crisis, press for the truth, insist on answers, and demand the strong checks and balances that are essential to the idea of America. One of the most important reasons our system of government is so successful, why our democracy has endured, is that we set limits on government power. Elected leaders and government bureaucrats are bounded by the Constitution, laws passed by Congress, and the availability of review of actions taken by independent courts staffed with impartial judges. Checks on power help guarantee that we stay a free country, but these important checks have been greatly eroded.

That is why Americans from all walks of life have stood up against actions by a handful of leaders and operatives who acted in secret and in violation of our laws—with practices like monitoring Americans without court warrants or any proof of wrongdoing, detaining people in secret prisons without redress by the courts, and torture. The Chairman was right to call for a truth commission to ensure that there is accountability to our system of government. Unfortunately, that common sense call has been rebuffed, and the vacuum left by the lack of accounting has been filled with self-serving claims that these policies "work." And, there has been precious little space to have a real conversation about better alternatives that would be both more effective and more consistent with needed checks and balances.

While some of the powers at issue allow people to be monitored without any proof of wrongdoing, the government always concedes that conducting surveillance of everyone is not possible or efficient. But that concession masks the true extent and the true costs of the massive web of secret surveillance of Americans that has been erected over the past several years. Due to the cloak of secrecy that envelopes these powers, it is difficult to picture what is really happening behind closed doors. And, we want to believe that government agents are focused only on the bad guys, but the record tells a different story. Not only does evidence show that many innocent Americans are being secretly swept in, but also the record shows this is happening *because* of recent changes to how the law is written or interpreted, not in spite of the law. Meanwhile, key facts have been kept hidden or been disclosed quite selectively, while other "facts" have turned out to be deliberately misleading, if not outright lies or propaganda. That is one of the reasons that while this debate is often cast in terms of the other, the enemy, it is more properly focused on what we stand *for* as a free people, what our rules should be for surveillance in *this* country, and whether we will call out misinformation and demand the truth as sovereign citizens.

II. The Current Patriot Act Debate and What Should Be on the Table

Today's hearing is focused on the three provisions designated by the Patriot Act reauthorization bill to be up for renewal this year: Section 215, secret orders for records or information about you held by third parties; Section 206, secret roving wiretaps; and the so-called "lone wolf" provision. Rather than adopt this format, I am going to focus on how some of the powers set to expire relate to broader issues at stake and other provisions that should be on the table. I simply do not think this White House and this Congress should accede to the agenda for this debate dictated by the Republican-controlled Congress and White House in 2006. Other secret surveillance powers that undermine Americans' privacy can and should be on the table, and so I would urge this Committee, this Congress, and the new Administration not to feel bound by the narrow topics teed up back in 2006 for debate today.

That is one of the reasons I am very appreciative of the Chairman's decision to include changes to the National Security Letter (NSL) provisions expanded by Section 505 of the Patriot Act and by the 2006 reauthorization, among others. I hope a majority of this Committee will support Senator Feingold's amendments to sensibly update the standards for issuing NSLs and revise other powers that are dangerously overbroad or unjustified, as detailed in his JUSTICE Act. (I am especially proud to be here as a new constituent of Senator Feingold, who bravely stood alone against Patriot in 2001.)

A. Domestic Surveillance that Undermines the Privacy of Americans' Personal Records

1. § 215 Orders Cover Any Tangible Thing and Require No Wrongdoing by You

One way to think of the scope of the power covered by Section 215 of the Patriot Act is to think of a giant file into which literally "any tangible thing" held by a third party about you can be put, that is, can be secretly obtained by government agents. Any tangible thing. It could be your DNA, your genetic code, from tests taken by your doctor for your health. It could be records about the books you buy or read. It could be information about websites you have visited. To search your home for these types of personal records, the government would have to have a warrant based on probable cause of wrongdoing, but to obtain them from your doctor or others you do business with, such as your internet service provider or your employer, no such probable cause is required under the statute since 2001.

In fact, any tangible thing about you can be secretly obtained without any evidence that you are a suspected terrorist. Virtually everything about you can be seized through secret 215 orders if you have any contact with a suspect. On the surface that might sound reasonable, but when you think it through you can see that every day through work or business you come into contact with dozens of people, at work, at schools, at conferences, in the cafeteria, at sporting events, at the mall, and if any one of them is the subject of an investigation your sensitive, personal private information might get swept up and kept in government files for decades. That amounts to hundreds of people a year and mere contact, however brief, can trigger this law, which requires the secret Foreign Intelligence Surveillance Court to presume your sensitive personal records are relevant to an investigation and grant a secret access.

And, under the law as amended in 2006, your employer, doctor, or librarian, for example, who may have known you since childhood, cannot ever tell you your privacy has been breached without going to court, even if you are never charged with any wrongdoing. And, it bars them from even challenging such orders for your personal, private information for a year. And, even then, the law as amended in 2006 makes it almost impossible for that person or business to prevail, by creating a conclusive presumption against disclosure if a government official certifies the request should be kept secret for various reasons, without providing the court with any facts to test such assertions.

It is no wonder that librarians and booksellers and other groups devoted to protecting freedom of conscience strongly oppose these far-reaching and excessive secret powers. At every juncture, the prior administration eliminated checks and balances that would help protect the innocent and ensure these powers were properly focused. Senator Leahy's bill would require that the government provide facts showing why they think the records they are seeking are actually relevant rather than just show any contact with a subject of an investigation, and it would allow recipients to challenge orders for the disclosure of any tangible thing sought. These changes would untie the court's hands in assessing the original request and any challenge to it or to the related gag order. Senator Feingold's bill would make similar changes and also require that any restriction on freedom of speech related to receiving such an order be narrowly tailored, in accordance with First Amendment law, and it would allow the use of these tangible things to be challenged in court just like any other evidence. Both bills would also require more court oversight of how the things obtained with these orders are used or disseminated.

These are important steps toward containing and refocusing this far-reaching power. In my view, to better protect innocent Americans, this power should be predicated on more than mere contact—it should require some reason to believe the subject is knowingly aiding a suspect rather than merely in the wrong place at the wrong time while engaged the innocent business of daily life. Congress should also probe the findings of the Inspector General that, after a rare denial of a requested Section 215 order, the FBI circumvented the court by using an NSL and should prevent this from happening again.

2. Extreme Secrecy Was Used to Obscure the Truth and Distort the Debate

The Section 215 power was subjected to a sunset, or time limit, back in 2001 because it was a newly created, far-reaching power. In the debate over the Patriot Act in 2005, the Bush Administration made a deliberate decision to voluntarily de-classify statistics about how infrequently this power was used. The power had been used only a few dozen times, and this fact was used to attack opponents as overreacting to the potential danger of this power. Since then, the government has used this power much more regularly, resulting in a ten-fold increase in Section 215 orders in just two years.

At the same time, the administration adamantly refused to disclose the number of demands for third party records being issued under the changes made by Section 505 of the Patriot Act, which is known as the National Security Letter (NSL) power. NSLs were not made subject to the sunset in 2005 because they were a power that pre-dated the Patriot Act, even though those powers were greatly expanded in 2001. One way to think about the relationship between Section 215 orders for any tangible thing and Section 505 demands for information about financial transactions, phone records, internet transactions (who you e-mail and who e-mails you), and credit reporting information is to think of a circle within a circle. Everything covered by a Section 505 demand also counts as a tangible thing under Section 215, but not every tangible thing is a financial, internet, phone, or credit record.

However, notwithstanding the dangers of permissive access to any tangible thing about you without any showing of probable cause, Section 505 NSLs are even more dangerous to individual liberty. This is because NSLs are issued by the FBI without any court approval whatsoever. These are unilateral, coercive, and secret demands by FBI agents to businesses for personal, private information about you, without even having to show the secret FISA court in Washington any evidence supporting the request. So, of course, we in the civil liberties community believed these powers were being widely used. And, even though this controversial power became a major part of the reauthorization debate in 2005, the administration refused to make public even the number of requests made, while touting the assertion that it had used the related Section 215 powers sparingly, only a handful of times. The ACLU filed a FOIA request for the numbers and ended up with six-page document in which nearly every entry related to the number of NSLs was redacted except for the words "Grand Total." It literally took an act of Congress to dislodge the information about how often NSLs had been used, through required audits and reporting, which were some of the only real improvements made in the deeply flawed 2006 reauthorization of the Patriot Act.

But, in November 2005 as the Patriot Act was being delayed by a mounting filibuster in the Senate, an investigative piece by the Washington Post's Bart Gellman quoted government sources reporting that the number of NSL requests had exploded to over 30,000 per year.[4] The Justice Department harshly attacked the article in a letter to then-Chairman Specter signed by William Moschella, and calling the 30,000 figure "inaccurate." I myself heard from a number of staff and reporters that the administration had absolutely denied that anywhere near this number of demands had been made, just as the NSL powers were being debated on the Hill and in public. Congress responded to the controversy by requiring an audit of the number of times the power was being used.

That is how in 2007 we learned that the true number of NSL requests issued in 2004, the year before the article was published, was over 56,000. [5] The number reported in the press was not too big; it was too small! The administration attempted to sidestep this dispute by asserting that its statements were based on counting only the number of letters and not the number of requests. Yet, administration officials had to know that individual letters often had multiple requests. To this day, there has been no real accountability for the way the public was misled by DOJ at the crucial moment in this debate. In another instance of deliberately distorting the public debate in 2005, while the prior administration was asserting that the government was not interested in library records it was simultaneously seeking records from the Library Connection in Connecticut and gagging those librarians from telling Congress and rebutting the misleading assertions of the government. Both the Leahy and Feingold bills amend the law to address the constitutional flaws noted by the U.S. Court of Appeals for the Second Circuit in that case regarding the gag order that accompanies an NSL. These improvements are essential.

3. Weakened Standards for NSLs Have Swept in Numerous Innocent People

The Department of Justice's own Annual Performance and Accountability Report in 2006 described in stark terms how the current standards for using NSLs affect ordinary Americans:

> Likewise, investigative and intelligence authorities enacted or expanded in the Patriot Act [and the 2005 reauthorization] invest broad new information-gathering powers in FBI agents and their supervisors . . . on a minimal evidentiary predicate. For example, . . . it authorized the FBI to collect information such as telephone records, Internet usage, and credit and banking information on persons who are not subjects of FBI investigations. This means that the FBI—and other law enforcement or Intelligence Community agencies with access to FBI databases—is able to review and

> store information about American citizens and others in the United States who are not subjects of FBI foreign counterintelligence investigations and about whom the FBI has no individualized suspicion of illegal activity.

www.usdoj.gov/ag/annualreports/pr2006/2006par.pdf (adding that therefore these powers need "aggressive oversight" internally).

The Feingold bill redresses this problem with an important update to NSLs to require the bare minimum that should be required in a free society: that the FBI have individualized suspicion about the person records it wants pertain to, instead of permitting an internal government assertion or boilerplate certification of relevance to an "authorized investigation." This is critically important because the Executive Branch re-wrote the rules to allow a "preliminary inquiry" to count as an authorized investigation, even though the statute intended that these intrusive powers only be used when a full investigation was underway, which required at least some evidence of a reasonable likelihood of wrongdoing. Even the FBI Director conceded to Senator Wyden in 2005 that these newly renamed "preliminary investigations" had "no particular standard of proof." (And, I would strongly urge the Committee to look more closely at the revised AG Guidelines for investigations, which also need to be changed to protect against increased monitoring of First Amendment activities.)

Under the current weakened "standard," as the Inspector General noted, the FBI has used NSLs to obtain information about people two or three degrees of separation away from the target/subject of an investigation. This is important for ensuring that these powers are sensibly focused. Assuming, conservatively, that an average person is in contact with a hundred people between family, friends, co-workers, and merchants, two degrees of separation is 10,000 people (100 x 100)—and, it is documented that one investigation in 2004 alone used a nine NSLs to obtain information about over 11,000 people. And, three degrees of separation could sweep in 100,000 people (10,000 x 100). It is far too permissive and unreasonable to allow these intrusive powers such a broad, almost arbitrary reach into Americans' lives and communities.

It is also the case that FBI agents told the Inspector General that NSLs were very useful in clearing people and closing files, but the FBI General Counsel has asserted that private records about people who are cleared be kept for perpetually, purportedly to help clear them again. Indeed, in 2007, the Inspector General made clear that nothing in DOJ or FBI policies require "the purging of information derived from NSLs in FBI databases, regardless of the outcome of the investigation. Thus, once information is obtained in response to a national security letter, it is indefinitely retained and retrievable by the many authorized personnel who have access to various FBI databases." How many of the people subject to the over NSL requests are innocent? We do not know for certain, but we do know that the government conducts only a couple dozen international terrorism prosecutions per year, according to the Transactional Records Access Clearinghouse.

4. The Number of NSL Requests Dwarf the Number of 215 Order

Cumulatively, we know that over 230,000 NSL requests have been issued in the past eight years, but even this number is too low. Despite receiving a personal assurance by the Director of the FBI that some reasonable estimate of the of NSLs issued in 2001 and 2002 would be made public, those numbers remain undisclosed. Plus, the figures reported for 2007 and 2008 exclude the number of NSL requests for internet transaction information. So, the true number could be 300,000, more or less.

Even that number would not include any NSLs that were withdrawn or threatened, as Gellman reported occurred when Las Vegas casinos shared over 1,000,000 hotel records in late 2003/early 2004. (Hotel/casinos were swept into the NSL powers when the law was amended to construe "financial institution" to include casinos, as well as insurance companies, jewelers, boat sellers, and the U.S. Postal Service, among other institutions that are not banks but that have some cash business.) Those figures are not included in the statistics, which demonstrates how even mandatory reporting about the mere numbers of NSLs can be sidestepped through other tools, such as "voluntary" compliance with requests, the use of grand jury subpoenas, and grounded or groundless assertions of emergency or exigency, none of which currently require public reporting and which should be fixed. This also underscores a little-noticed fact that has emerged: NSLs are not the exclusive means for obtaining Americans' financial, credit, internet, or phone records. This creates uncertainty for agents and a real lack of adequate controls to protect the public. Fortunately, the Feingold bill includes a provision to ensure that the FBI's unlawful use of so-called exigent letters is barred and emergencies are bona fide.

Even assuming the 230,000 figure were not significantly understated, the number of 215 orders is dwarfed by the number of NSL demands. At a minimum, there are almost a thousand NSLs issued for every 215 order issued. NSLs are affecting tens of thousands more people in the U.S. than Section 215 orders, and yet the focus on the expiring powers is effectively distracting from the more widely used NSLs. Additionally, NSLs are being used increasingly against United States citizens who now represent the majority of individuals about whom and NSL has been issued. (In 2006, 60% of NSLs were about U.S. persons, compared with approximately a third in 2003.)

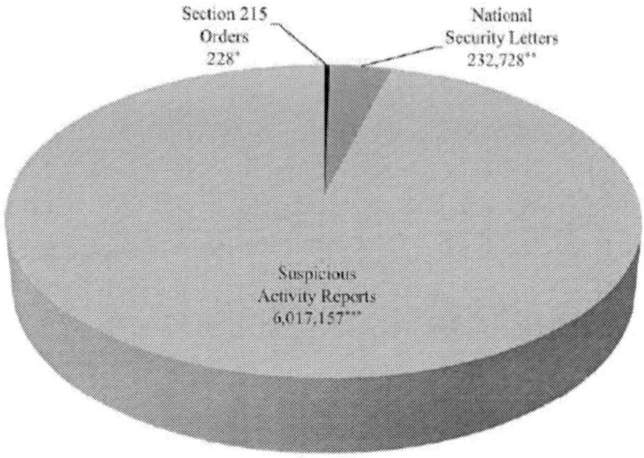

Section 215 Represents a Tiny Slice of the Data FBI Is Now Collecting

Sources for chart data (with thanks to the ACLU's recent report on the Patriot Act):

* U.S. DEP'T OF JUSTICE, OFFICE OF INSPECTOR GENERAL, A REVIEW OF THE FEDERAL BUREAU OF INVESTIGATION'S USE OF SECTION 215 ORDERS FOR BUSINESS RECORDS 77 (Mar. 2007), available at http://www.usdoj.gov/oig/special/ s0703a/final.pdf (number of Section 215 orders in 2001 through 2005); U.S. DEP'T OF JUSTICE, OFFICE OF INSPECTOR GENERAL, A REVIEW OF THE FBI'S USE OF SECTION 215 ORDERS FOR BUSINESS RECORDS IN 2006, 84 (Mar. 2008), available at http://www.usdoj.gov/oig/special/s0803a/final.pdf (number of Section 215 orders in 2006); Letter from Brian A. Benczkowski, Principal Deputy Assistant Attorney General, U.S. Department of Justice, to Nancy Pelosi, Speaker, U.S. House of Representatives (Apr. 30, 2008), available at *http://www.fas.org* /irp/ agency/doj/fisa/2007rept.pdf (number of Section 215 orders in 2007); Letter from Ronald Weich, Assistant Attorney General, U.S. Department of Justice, to Harry Reid, Majority Leader, U.S. Senate (May 14, 2009), available at http://www.fas.org/irp/ agency/doj/fisa/2008rept.pdf (number of Section 215 orders in 2008).

** See U.S. DEP'T OF JUSTICE, OFFICE OF INSPECTOR GENERAL, A REVIEW OF THE FEDERAL BUREAU OF INVESTIGATION'S USE OF NATIONAL SECURITY LETTERS 37, 120 (Mar. 2007), *available at* http://www.usdoj.gov/oig/special/s0703b/final.pdf (number of NSL requests in 2000 through 2005); U.S. DEP'T OF JUSTICE, OFFICE OF INSPECTOR GENERAL, A REVIEW OF THE FBI'S USE OF NATIONAL SECURITY LETTERS: ASSESSMENT OF CORRECTIVE ACTIONS AND EXAMINATION OF NSL USAGE IN 2006, 107 (Mar. 2008), available at http://www.usdoj.gov

/oig/special/s0803b/final.pdf (number of NSL requests in 2006); Letter from Ronald Weich, Assistant Attorney General, U.S. Department of Justice, to Harry Reid, Majority Leader, U.S. Senate (May 14, 2009), available at http://www.fas.org/irp/agency/doj/fisa/2008rept.pdf (number of NSL requests in 2007 and 2008).

*** U.S. DEP'T OF THE TREASURY, FINANCIAL CRIMES ENFORCEMENT NETWORK, THE SAR ACTIVITY REVIEW – BY THE NUMBERS, ISSUE 12, 4 (June 2009), *available at* http://www.fincen.gov/news_room/rp/files/sar_by_numb_12.pdf.

5. And, the Number of NSLs Is Dwarfed by Suspicious Activity Reports

Title III of the Patriot Act expanded immunity and incentives for financial institutions to secretly file Suspicious Activity Reports (SARs) on their customers. SARs are sent from banks, for example, to the U.S. Department of the Treasury, which transmits these reports to the FBI for inclusion in the Investigative Data Warehouse. Even though SARs are not issued by the government, they are part of the broader issues resulting in the tremendous expansion in FBI files about ordinary Americans. Most of the hearings about this issue have featured government witnesses talking about connecting the dots and stopping the flow of terrorist money. But, little has been done to examine the exponential growth in the number of private financial records being secretly and voluntarily shared with the government. Back in 2000, the number of SARs was about 160,000 per year, and the annual figure has increased ten-fold in less than a decade, with over 1.2 million issued in 2007 alone.

Plainly, the majority of Americans who have now had the personal, financial information involuntarily turned over to the federal government through the voluntary actions of their banks have not been charged with any wrongdoing. But, these records will stay in the federal databases indefinitely. Even though the Senate Judiciary Committee does not have primary jurisdiction over FinCEN matters, it should explore how these powers relate to the demands for financial information with NSLs.

Financial records now represent a significant component of the FBI's data "warehouse," which reported having almost 1 billion records as of late 2008. That is three times more records than people in the U.S. As the Electronic Frontier Foundation has noted, that is more records than are held by the largest library in the world, the Library of Congress, which has "138 million items in its collection."[6] As Bart Gellman reported in 2005, the Investigative Data Warehouse only began five years ago, in 2004, and already it has accumulated a billion records. If the number of records contained in the IDW were compared to the pie chart on the prior page, the IDW pie would be 50 times larger. Yet, there has been almost no public examination or hearings focused on this gargantuan database. And the IDW is focused primarily on U.S. records and people in the U.S. The FBI has a whole separate data warehouse, the Foreign Terrorist Tracking Task Force (FTTTF) "Datamart," for foreign terrorism investigations focused abroad, and that database has even more records in it than the IDW.

Additionally, despite revelations by Mr. Gellman and others, there has been no public examination of how the FBI is using contracts it has with the databroker ChoicePoint or with LexisNexis' financial assets databases to obtain or verify and obtain information about Americans. It is certainly the case that the Executive Branch has elsewhere said that it is determined to exploit so-called "open source" data and that the government has a right to information that commercial companies have, but it is not clear precisely what rules the FBI is operating under when its agents access ChoicePoint, for example, or how this relates to compelling versus voluntary disclosures by traditional financial institutions under NSLs or 215 orders or other claimed authority. It is also not clear how much taxpayer money is going into these contracts and what meaningful privacy protections, if any, are being applied. There is no information about how much private companies may be profiting by selling access to this data to the federal government. And, there has been no reporting about how many Americans have had information about them that may have been accumulated by ChoicePoint accessed by the government. And, the public has a right to know the answers to these questions.

These issues may seem complicated on the surface, but they are really about a fundamental question in a democracy: how much information should the government be able to accumulate about a person, without any evidence of any wrongdoing. I would submit that the answer should be very little, but it seems the government thinks the answer should be almost unlimited. And, nowadays, there is no need to create a separate file on a particular person when all the data can easily be aggregated at the touch of a button through the use of internal search engines that can accumulate information about a person.

B. Section 206 and Related Secret Wiretapping Needed Reforms

Just as the discussion of Section 215 of the Patriot Act implicates other powers with broader impact on individual privacy, Section 206 cannot be reasonably understood without reference to FISA powers. Before news broke that President Bush violated federal laws requiring judicial approval to conduct electronic surveillance in the US in investigations to prevent terrorism, he misled the American people, telling Marylanders and Ohioans in 2005 that the government "needs a federal judge's permission to wiretap a foreign terrorist's phone, a federal judge's permission to track his calls...." Back in 2004, in an effort to blunt controversy about his powers, President Bush assured New Yorkers: "Any time you hear the United States government talking about a wiretap, it requires—a wiretap requires a court order. Nothing has changed, by the way. When we're talking about chasing down terrorists, we're talking about getting a court order before we do so."

Once Eric Lichtblau and James Risen of the New York Times broke the story about the extraordinary electronic surveillance the administration was engaging in without warrants and in violation of the law, President Bush and his aides claimed that he was not misleading because he was talking about the Patriot Act's roving wiretap provisions. But, that was just more misinformation. The false implication was that the Patriot Act was totally separate from the laws the administration had broken. The Patriot Act amended the law President Bush broke but did not repeal the requirement of individualized judicial warrants for terrorism wiretaps.

Indeed, before the story broke, even the President's own advisors used to concede: "the primary provision in the Patriot Act makes amendments to the Foreign Intelligence Surveillance Act [FISA], which is the secret court you hear about that issues secret wiretaps. . . for over 25 years that have been tested in the courts that strike the proper balance between expanding our fight against terrorism, but protecting civil liberties at the same time." This is what John Yoo, former Bush appointee in DOJ's Office of Legal Counsel, told this to CNN in 2005. Yet, Mr. Yoo knew the administration was not following these rules because Mr. Yoo helped write the memos that rationalized evading the very requirements he was extolling on national television.

The suggestion that these binding laws somehow do not apply to terrorism ignores the plain language of the laws that were broken. It is important to recall that the Bush Administration asked for, and Congress passed, several amendments to the electronic surveillance provisions of FISA in the Patriot Act, which is titled "Providing Appropriate Tools Required to Intercept and Obstruct Terrorism." And FISA expressly constituted the "exclusive" rules for foreign intelligence surveillance in the US, including electronic surveillance to prevent "international terrorism," making it a crime to wiretap without court approval.

Under classic FISA, it does not matter whether the wiretaps involve multiple phones, known as multi-point or "roving" wiretaps, or involve just one phone. Federal law requires judicial approval for all electronic surveillance of Americans. To accept the assertions would require accepting the false claim that the only time judges are required is when the person tapped is using more than one phone. The law required individual warrants no matter how few or how many phones or email accounts are tapped.

Until last year, FISA required that the government identify the telephone or device to be tapped in a secret wiretap order. But, with last year's passage of the FISA Amendments Act (FAA), the government is not required to disclose to the court the "facility" where the acquisition of electronic information takes place, let alone particular phones, for surveillance that meets the FAA's test. So, the Section 206 rules that permit what have become known as "John Doe roving wiretaps" apply to a narrow category of cases within the U.S. that are not covered by the broad orders for electronic surveillance of international communications that are permitted under the FAA, orders that I and others believe are unconstitutional. That is why I support not just Senator Feingold's amendments to cure the flaws in the roving wiretap powers, but also the much needed changes he proposes to the revised FISA authorities. I support Senator Feingold's amendments in Title III of his bill to address these issues.

The amendment against bulk collection is particularly important because of the way the FISA Amendments Act could be construed and especially in light of the "over-collection" revelations earlier this year. Additionally, I know that the FISA Amendments Act attempted to bar using blanket orders for electronic collection from being used to acquire purely domestic communications. However, President Bush and his allies inserted language in the bill making the bar on collecting domestic calls or e-mails applicable only when the government knows "at the time of acquisition" that the sender and all recipients are physically located in the U.S. This weasel language permits ignorance to be bliss when it comes to rules intended to protect purely domestic calls or emails. The other amendments in Title III are also important and would help restore civil liberties in this country.

Even though there is little political appetite to revisit the FISA rules, I think doing so is important in the context of the Patriot reauthorization debate. For example, the public has never received a clear answer about the published reports that FBI agents were distracted by ineffective and wasteful surveillance leads generated from the NSA's illegal electronic surveillance program.[7] Here is part of that report:

> In the anxious months after the Sept. 11 attacks, the National Security Agency began sending a steady stream of telephone numbers, e-mail addresses and names to the F.B.I. in search of terrorists. The stream soon became a flood, requiring hundreds of agents to check out thousands of tips a month. But virtually all of them, current and former officials say, led to dead ends or innocent Americans. . . . "We'd chase a number, find it's a school teacher with no indication they've ever been involved in international terrorism - case closed," said one former FBI official, who was aware of the program and the data it generated for the bureau. "After you get a thousand numbers and not one is turning up anything, you get some frustration."

As Suzanne Spaulding has previously suggested, and Kate Martin and I have repeatedly urged, we need a comprehensive examination of the domestic surveillance authorities and uses. Until this kind of far-ranging review is complete, the American people will be stuck with a patchwork of authorities that serve neither liberty nor security well.

C. Other Powers in Need of Reform

In addition to these powers, I would urge Congress to take a closer look at Section 213 of the Patriot Act, which granted sneak and peek powers in routine criminal cases, overwhelmingly in cases that have nothing to do with terrorism. I would also urge that the Committee take another look at the so-called "lone wolf" provision, which has reportedly not be used by the government, as well as other provisions addressed in Senator Feingold's set of amendments.

I would also like to commend Senator Leahy again for the base bill he has introduced on this issue, and all he has done and continues to do to defend individual rights and support common-sense improvements to the law. I understand that there is precious little time to resolve all these issues before the end of this Session of Congress, but I urge that these issues be examined and be resolved publicly to the extent possible.

Thank you again for the invitation and for considering my views.

End Notes

[1] I previously served as Deputy Director of the Center for National Security Studies (CNSS), the Senior Legislative Strategist for the American Civil Liberties Union (ACLU), the Chief Nominations Counsel for Senator Leahy, the Deputy Chief of the Article III Judges Division of the U.S. Courts, and Deputy Assistant Attorney General in the Office of Legal Policy/Office of Policy Development at the U.S. Department of Justice. I am indebted to the work of my former colleagues with the ACLU—Michelle Richardson, Mike German, and Jeani Murray of the legislative office and Ann Beeson, Jameel Jaffer, Melissa Goodman who were litigating these issues during my tenure there, among other devoted civil libertarians—my former partner, Kate Martin, of CNSS who has been challenging these issues since before 2001, intelligence expert Suzanne Spaulding whom I am testifying alongside today, and other great civil liberties advocates in the national security surveillance coalition I have helped lead since the 2005 debate over Patriot Act reauthorization and in the ongoing challenges to warrantless wiretapping. I would also like to thank Kate Rhudy for her assistance with this testimony and all her help over the past two years as my law clerk and now as a lawyer. My testimony reflects my own views, of course, and any mistakes are my own.

[2] The Center for Media and Democracy, which was founded by John Stauber in 1993, is an independent, non-profit, non-partisan public interest organization dedicated to promoting transparency and informed debate by exposing government propaganda and corporate spin. Among our priorities is countering misinformation by investigating public relations campaigns by the government and informing grassroots citizen activism that promotes human rights as well as other policies to make the world a better place. CMD's investigations have been praised by leading journalists, such as Amy Goodman of Democracy Now! who observed that "The Center's work in exposing government and corporate propaganda is absolutely essential to our democracy."

[3] Quoted by Andrew Sullivan in THE ATLANTIC, "Dear President Bush" (October 2009).

[4] Barton Gellman, "The FBI's Secret Scrutiny: In Hunt for Terrorists, Bureau Examines Records of Ordinary Americans" WASHINGTON POST, A01 (Sunday, November 6, 2005).

[5] For my detailed assessment of the 2007 NSL audit, *see* www.intelligence.house.gov /Media/PDFS/Graves032807.pdf.

[6] http://www.eff.org/issues/foia/investigative-data-warehouse-report. For a comprehensive examination of the IDW, access EFF's report.

[7] Lowell Bergman, Eric Lichtblau, Scott Shane and Don Van Natta Jr., "Spy Agency Data After Sept. 11 Led F.B.I. to Dead Ends," THE NEW YORK TIMES (January 17, 2006).

CHAPTER SOURCES

The following Chapters have been previously published:

Chapter 1- This is an edited reformatted and augmented version of a Congressinal Research Service publication, report R40980, dated March 2, 2010.-

Chapter 2- This is an edited reformatted and augmented version of a Congressinal Research Service publication, report, RL33424, dated February 2, 2010.

Chapter 3- These remarks were delivered as testimony given on September 23, 2009. Glenn A. Fine, Inspectore General, U.S. Department of Justice before the Senate Sub Committee on the Judiciary.

Chapter 4- These remarks were delivered as testimony given on September 23, 2009. Lisa Graves, Executive Director for the Center for Media and Democracy before the United States Senate Judiciary Committee

.

INDEX

9

A

B

C

M

N

O

P

Q

R

S